CRITICAL STUDIES IN BLACK LIFE
AND CULTURE
VOL. 29

LANGSTON HUGHES

GARLAND REFERENCE LIBRARY OF THE
HUMANITIES
VOL. 1872

CRITICAL STUDIES IN BLACK LIFE AND CULTURE

C. JAMES TROTMAN
General Editor

LANGSTON HUGHES

The Man, His Art, and His Continuing Influence

edited by

C. James Trotman
With Keynote Essay by
Arnold Rampersad

Emery Wimbish, Jr.
Project Director
Lincoln University

GARLAND PUBLISHING, Inc.
New York & London / 1995

Conference proceedings held at Lincoln University in Pennsylvania on March 26, 27, and 28, 1992, with support provided by the National Endowment for the Humanities to Lincoln University's Langston Hughes Memorial Library

Copyright © 1995 by C. James Trotman
All rights reserved

Allen County Public Library
900 Webster Street
PO Box 2270
Fort Wayne, IN 46801-2270

Library of Congress Cataloging-in-Publication Data

Langston Hughes : the man, his art, and his continuing influence / C. James Trotman, editor ; with keynote essay by Arnold Rampersad.
    p. cm. — (Critical studies in Black life and culture ; vol. 29) (Garland reference library of the humanities ; vol. 1872)
    "Conference proceedings held at Lincoln University in Pennsylvania on March 26, 27, and 28, 1992."
    Includes bibliographical references and index.
    ISBN 0-8153-1763-8
    1. Hughes, Langston, 1902–1967—Criticism and interpretation—Congresses. 2. Afro-Americans in literature—Congresses. 3. Harlem (New York, N.Y.)—Intellectual life—Congresses. 4. Harlem Renaissance—Congresses. I. Trotman, C. James, 1943– . II. Series. III. Series: Critical studies on Black life and culture ; v. 29.
PS3515.U274Z6733 1995
818'.5209—dc20   95-15708
                                          CIP

Cover illustration: Portrait of Langston Hughes. Drawing by Mrs. Grace B. Rivero. Courtesy of the artist.

Printed on acid-free, 250-year-life paper
Manufactured in the United States of America

THIS BOOK IS DEDICATED
TO LANGSTON HUGHES, OUR KEEPER OF DREAMS LIVED AND DEFERRED
TO EMERY WIMBISH, JR., CULTURAL TRUSTEE
TO THE ASSEMBLED SCHOLARS AND LIBRARIANS
FOR ANITA, THANE, AND BRAEDEN

Contents

General Editor's Preface

Critical Studies in Black Life and Culture is a series devoted to original, book-length studies of African American developments. Written by well-qualified scholars, the series is interdisciplinary and global, interpreting tendencies and themes wherever African Americans have left their mark. The ideal reader for the series is one who appreciates the combined use of scholarly inquiry with a focus on a people whose roots stretch around the world.

Critical Studies is also a window to that world. The series holds out the promise of fulfilling the ideal of all scholarship by uncovering and disseminating the sources of a people's life-line. In relationship to this series, the untranslated Ghanaan narratives offering the earliest perspectives on African life and thought illustrate a scholarly need in this area. If and when they are published, we might have a clearer view of the past and of the consciousness of blacks in antiquity. The clarity would almost certainly contribute to a more detailed basis for understanding what the roots of "culture" and "civilization" are for African Americans in particular and for all of us in general.

Sometimes, however, the scholarly works published in Critical Studies remind us that the windows have not always been open or, if they were, the shades were pulled down, making it difficult if not impossible to see in or out. The series reaffirms forerunners who, by talent and determination, refused to be unseen or unheard: Phillis Wheatley, Anna Julia Cooper, Frederick Douglass, William E.B. DuBois, Zora Neale Hurston, Langston Hughes, and Ralph Ellison. They laid the aesthetic and intellectual foundation for Ralph Bunche, Albert Luthuli, Desmond Tutu, Martin Luther King, Jr., Wole Soyinka, and Toni Morrison to be awarded Nobel prizes. In addition to individual achievements, the outstanding examples of organized and permanent group life are to be found in the historic black church, black colleges and universities, and the NAACP; none of these, I might add, has received a comprehensive historical treatment, leaving sizeable gaps in any effort to conceptualize a total picture of multicultural America.

All of these achievements suggest a promising future in African American developments, pointing to a great deal of activity—some from those who have successfully peeked around pulled-down shades to look out, while others have found ways to peep in. Critical Studies in Black Life and Culture is committed to publishing the best scholarship on African American life.

C. James Trotman
West Chester University

Contributors

Sophy H. Cornwell
Special Collections Librarian (retired)
Lincoln University

Thadious M. Davis
Professor of English
Brown University

Ella Forbes
Assistant Professor of African American Studies
Temple University

Sandra Y. Govan
Associate Professor of English
University of North Carolina—Charlotte

Donna Akiba Sullivan Harper
Associate Professor of English
Spelman College

Joyce Ann Joyce
Professor of English
Chicago State University

Bruce Kellner
Professor Emeritus of English
Millersville University

Kristin Hunter-Lattany
Senior Lecturer Emeritus of English
University of Pennsylvania

R. Baxter Miller
Professor of English and Director of African American Studies
University of Georgia

Thomas C. Phelps
Program Officer
Humanities Projects in Libraries and Archives
Division of Public Programs
National Endowment for the Humanities

Arnold Rampersad
Woodrow Wilson Professor of Literature and Director
of American Studies
Princeton University

Ropo Sekoni
Professor of English
Lincoln University

Niara Sudarkasa
President
Lincoln University

Steven C. Tracy
Assistant Professor
University of Massachusetts at Amherst

C. James Trotman
Professor of English
West Chester University

Cheryl A. Wall
Associate Professor of English
Rutgers University

Emery Wimbish, Jr.
Professor/Head Librarian
Lincoln University

Langston Hughes

A P(a)lace for Langston Hughes

C. James Trotman

West Chester University

The idea of a place, a setting, a physical or imagined space that becomes symbolic of human actions and interests is a pervasive concept running throughout this volume of conference papers, dedicated to the life and artistry of James Mercer Langston Hughes (1902–1967) on the twenty-fifth anniversary of his death. It is a fitting representation. With an energetic imagination and longevity to match, Hughes appears always to have anchored his literary art in places that general readers and scholars attach themselves to with relative ease. Part of the art of Hughes was to make the known available, begin a journey in a familiar spot here and there but end it with a reader or observer being transformed from witness to participant, from critic to sympathizer, maybe even collaborator, and from conditions of alienation to finding a personal shrine, a palace as such, to fulfill one's self in a world where that is increasingly hard to do.

"The Negro Artist and the Racial Mountain Top" was such an early place for Hughes. An imaginary lookout post, a lighthouse of sorts, this essay first appeared in the *Nation* in 1926. It was an artistic manifesto in which Hughes voiced the independent integrity of the black artist, an important concept at any time but historically representative of the *zeitgeist* of this century's first quarter. This was a tumultuous epoch roaring with revolutionary militancy from Petrograd and Paris to the Negro Renaissance in America. Moreover, the image of the artist

3

standing almost, but not quite existentially, aloof on a peak with racial markers, embraces so many of our impressions and understanding about creative artists, their works, and our responses to them. The fusion of experiences and devices of art, the imaginative uses of facts and fictions, the private and public wanderings are well-known scenes in the artist's *rite de passage*. When thinking about Hughes's life, his work, and his influence in this context, we begin another celebrated journey. Part of his drawing power as a belletrist is to be found in the variety of these sojourns.

Hughes was a peripatetic artist. On a global scale, his own international travels began in 1923 when he went to Africa and, later, to Europe in the same year. As readers we are drawn with him into symbolic, ancestral reflections in "The Negro Speaks of Rivers" (1921) and into autobiographical accounts of these travels recorded later in *The Big Sea* (1940). Sounds, particularly the musical quality of words, pulled him into the cultural repository of African American music where he used the blues for lyric poetry. In doing so, he expanded the American prosodic expression by incorporating this expressive folk form into the distinctive Afro-American voices found in *The Weary Blues* (1926), his first collection of poetry. But far more fundamental to Hughes's art was that language was a creative source for drawing with exquisite clarity and compassion the lives, manners, and customs of black folk.

In dramatic plays like *Mulatto* and *Mule Bone* (with Negro Renaissance's *femme noir* Zora Neale Hurston) he represented collisions between class and color consciousness—and one suspects some self-revelation too. In *The Simple Stories*, spun from Afro-American folk personalities for the daily productions of syndicated journalism, he recorded the sound of humor and the verbal dexterity that teases and often mocks our sober and presumed more systematic discoveries of life's secrets. It is very clear to anyone reading Hughes that the epic and worldly experiences of the African around the globe were both subjects for his art and sources of inspiration as well. If life versus art is a tension-filled dialectic full of potential debate for many theorists, Hughes's work makes it difficult to be reductive in this way. "Just be simple" is a pun of considerable sophistication: it is a life dictum and also a modern way of approaching the complexity present in Hughes's art.

The essays in this volume do in fact cast considerable fresh light on Hughesian scholarship. They move it toward a greater theoretical appreciation for his art and for the complexities of his personality that gave his art its special qualities. Part of that texture is derived, of course, from the African American experience. Hughes is partly responsible for the explosion of serious study of African American literary and cultural studies, especially about his peers and those who influenced his generation.

Since his death on May 22, 1967, there has been an impressive body of scholarship on Hughes, his contemporaries, and revisionist social history. Nathan Huggin's *Harlem Renaissance* (1971) pummels the period's walls of mainstream intellectual silence, followed shortly by Robert Hemenway's *Zora Neale Hurston: A Literary Biography* (1977), David L. Lewis's *When Harlem Was in Vogue* (1981)—and most recently his biography, *W.E.B. Du Bois, The Biography of a Race* (1993)—Wayne Cooper's *Claude McKay: Rebel Sojourner in the Harlem Renaissance* (1987), Martin Bernal's two volumes of *Black Athena: The Afroasiatic Roots of Classical Civilization* (1987), Martin Duberman's *Paul Robeson* (1988). No list would be complete—and this does not intend to be comprehensive—that failed to include the important critical study by Faith Berry, *Langston Hughes: Before and Beyond Harlem* (1983) and the watershed, critically acclaimed two-volume biographical studies by Arnold Rampersad of the Negro Renaissance's prolific son. In *The Life of Langston Hughes* (I and II 1986 and 1988), Rampersad created a more demanding standard for reading Hughes and for appreciating him.

Each of these scholarly books, in addition to the exceptional periodical essays in journals like *Callaloo*, expand upon a special place in the continuing explication of African American cultural history. Hughes kept this space alive. He gave it a warmth from which a light illuminated to guide the wayward to a port of call where the artist's honest labor exists; it might also serve to keep away the disabling darkness of evils, especially the persistent and mutating forms of racism from swallowing us all. Maybe this is part of his meaning when he wrote in his first published poem in 1921, "The Negro Speaks of Rivers," saying with all the assurance of a rich talent heralding his presence for all time, "I've known rivers older than the flow of human blood in human veins/My soul has grown deep like the rivers. . . ."

As a setting for this conference, Lincoln University is itself significant in any consideration of place in Hughes. The historical contributions of Africans to the world is to be found here and that of the African American imprint as a historic black college to the development of American higher education. Founded in 1854, this campus in the rolling hills of southeastern Pennsylvania anchors its identity in an alumni that bespeaks of worldwide leadership, with Hughes in the class of 1929 being one of its distinguished alumni that includes the late Supreme Court Justice Thurgood Marshall, the Ghanaan President Kwame Nkrumah, and countless stories of successful professionals in all walks of life.

In his keynote address to the conference, Professor Rampersad illustrates the young poet's awareness of a life committed to being a poet/writer and to joining a community of achievers at Lincoln. Rampersad read Hughes's October 20, 1925, admissions letter to Lincoln in which the young poet declared his commitment to a writer's life, citing the places where his writings were already in print. Clearly, he had plans to do more. The letter points this out and demonstrated Hughes's sense of personal vision, his early commitment to a writer's work, and the confidence of a young talent who was working his way through personal growth into finding his own place and destiny in the world of art "in order to be more useful to my race and America." Lincoln University has remembered Hughes appropriately and with affection by naming the university's library in his honor, an apostrophe for the poet laureate, that is directed by Professor Emery Wimbish, Jr., who initiated the call for this conference.

In his inimitable way, Hughes made spatial connectedness a paean for human affairs that is as much as any other component of his work a moral imperative for his art, his life, and his continuing influence. The work space for this continuing expressiveness is a place that in the final analysis is a great big edifice enabling us all, and together, to tell our stories. In this volume of essays, Hughes's life and work opens the doors, beginning—to take a phrase from his poem—by saying "I, too, sing."

Lincoln University Conference

3 1833 02839 5108

Langston Hughes:
The Man and the Writer, An Introduction

Emery Wimbish, Jr.
Project Director, Lincoln University

Poet, dramatist, short-story writer, translator, activist, and social critic, Langston Hughes is regarded by many as a major figure in American letters. Perhaps he is best remembered as one of the moving figures of the Harlem Renaissance, which included fellow poets Claude McKay and Countee Cullen as well as folklorist Zora Neale Hurston.

In March 1992, to mark the twenty-fifth anniversary of Hughes's death, a National Endowment for the Humanities (NEH) series of public programs on his life and work was presented at Lincoln University, Lincoln University, Pennsylvania, and the Chester County District Library in Exton, Pennsylvania.

It was especially fitting that Lincoln University should provide major conference facilities for introducing and enhancing the contributions of Langston Hughes as an internationally known writer. Of Hughes's recollection of Lincoln University, Dr. Arnold Rampersad in the first volume of his prize-winning biography *The Life of Langston Hughes* says:

> "Lincoln is wonderful," he wrote to Countee Cullen after a week at the little university of just over 300 students located amidst "trees and rolling hills and plenty of country" about forty-five miles southwest of Philadelphia. Life was "crude," but comfortable, the food "plain and solid:" there was "nothing out here but the school and therefore

the place has a spirit of its own, and it makes you feel as
though you 'belonged,' a feeling new to me because I
never seemed to belong anywhere." For the first time since
the segregated third grade in Kansas, Hughes was in
school among his own people. His first impressions were
all favorable. "Out here with the trees and rolling hills and
open sky, in old clothes, and this do-as-you-please atmo-
sphere, I rest content." After three weeks he was still
happy: "I like Lincoln so well, that I expect to be about six
years in graduating." (125)

An added advantage for having Lincoln University as the
major site was that it set the stage for the implementation of an
exemplary conference goal: "to promote awareness and use of
Hughes's personal library and memorabilia." These valuable
resources, which are housed in the library named in his memory,
are crucial to scholarship and research.

The critical essays included in this volume provide an in-
depth exploration of the theme of the conference: "Langston
Hughes: The Man and the Writer." The format adopted during
the planning phase was a lecture/discussion series with
supplementary displays of books, documents, manuscripts, and
other archival materials from Special Collections in Langston
Hughes Memorial Library. Dr. Rampersad delivered the keynote
address, entitled "The Man, the Writer, and His Continuing
Influence."

Other essays from the Panel Discussion sessions by "toilers
in the field" (in Dr. Rampersad's words) were:

Panel I—The Harlem Renaissance
Panel II—Hughes's Poetry and Music
Panel III—Race, Culture, Gender
Panel IV—The Fiction of Langston Hughes
Remarks on Hughes's Personal Library and Exhibits
Dramatic Retrospective—Performance by Freedom Theatre,
"Langston Hughes, Dramatist" (showcasing excerpts from the
dramatic oeuvre of Langston Hughes) by writer and director,
Gail Leslie.

These proceedings serve as a partial record of the conference and provide scholarly documentation to the public for ex-
panding its awareness of the work of Langston Hughes. The

majority of the humanities scholars included in this collection are well-known literary figures who brought special perspectives of Hughes. Some knew him, and this added a personal dimension that was engaging to the audience.

Included also is a partially biographical portrait of Langston Hughes and an introduction of the entire proceedings by President Niara Sudarkasa.

For the planning of the conference, special mention must be made of the members of the Advisory Board for their active participation during this period. I am extremely grateful to these Board members for their knowledgeable contributions: Dr. Thomas Battle, Dr. Charles Blockson, Mrs. Sophy Cornwell, Dr. Ezra Engling, Dr. Ella Forbes, Dr. Floyd Hardy, Dr. Jennifer Jordan, Dr. Arnold Rampersad, Mrs. Diane Silver, and Dr. C. James Trotman.

During the implementation phase of the project, the Advisory Committee was very helpful. This committee was composed of Ms. Lisa Bacon, Mrs. Sophy Cornwell, Mr. Claude Falcone, Dr. Ella Forbes, Mrs. Gail Leslie, Mrs. Mary Alice Lyons, Dr. Thomas Phelps, Mr. Donald Pierce, Dr. Arnold Rampersad, Ms. Ruth Schachter, Mrs. Diane Silver, Ms. Sue Smock, Dr. J. Paul Stephens, and Dr. C. James Trotman.

At the end of the conference, a questionnaire was distributed to participants to evaluate its success in meeting the goals established for the project. Although most made favorable comments, some were disappointed that there was not enough time for discussion and interaction with the audience.

Finally, I believe that the conference made a significant contribution to learning in the humanities through a critical examination of Hughes's work. Shown also in this series of programs is Langston Hughes's deep love of humanity, and it would behoove us to remember the words of one of his poems, "My People":

> The night is beautiful,
> So the faces of my people.
>
> The stars are beautiful,
> So the eyes of my people.

Beautiful, also, is the sun.
Beautiful, also, are the souls of my people.

This beautiful poem embodies for me the theme central to
the humanities conference: "Langston Hughes: The Man and the
Writer."

In Celebration of Langston Hughes

Niara Sudarkasa

President, Lincoln University

*To Professor Emery Wimbish whose affection, admiration, and respect
for Langston Hughes and dedicated service to Lincoln University led
him to conceptualize and organize this historic conference;*

*To all those at Lincoln, at the Chester County District Library
and elsewhere who worked with him to put together this exciting celebration of Langston Hughes, the Man and the Writer;*

*To the National Endowment for the Humanities, whose sponsor-
ship of the Conference made it possible;*

*To all the scholars, artists, and performers who, over the next
two days, will provide information, insight, ideas, and impressions
about Langston Hughes, the Man and the Writer;*

*To the Lincoln University faculty, staff, and students as well as
to all the visitors who have come to our campus to imbibe of the essence
of Langston Hughes as we partake of this intellectual feast provided by
those who know genius of the man and his works;*

*To our distinguished keynote speaker, Dr. Arnold Rampersad,
whose absorbing, poignant, and tasteful two-volume autobiography of
Langston Hughes made the man, his associates, his environment, and
his creative impulse come alive for me:*

Greetings and salutations. Welcome to Lincoln University, and
thank you for lending your presence to this splendid occasion. I
am exhilarated because you are here. I am excited about this con-

ference. I look forward to taking part in as many of the
conference events as possible.

How can I, as President of Lincoln University, say enough
in praise of Langston Hughes?

The reputation of every university is made by its faculty
and validated, vindicated, or vitiated by its alumni. Lincoln
University is fortunate in that its Founders created a reputation
for excellence and its alumni gave it the mark of distinction.

On the Lincoln University alumni roster, which reads like
an International Who's Who of the Twentieth Century, it is
generally agreed that there are four standouts, even among the
other giants: Langston Hughes of the Class of 1929, Thurgood
Marshall and Nnamdi Azikiwe of the Class of 1930, and Kwame
Nkrumah of the Class of 1939. It is very interesting that the first
three men were academic contemporaries here at Lincoln.

Certainly, the names of all four of them have been chiseled
in the granite of history, and none shall be forgotten so long as
the twentieth century itself is remembered. But had I to say that
any one of them "belongs to the ages," I would choose Langston
Hughes. Poets have a way of outlasting politicians and public
officials.

Geoffrey Chaucer, the fourteenth-century English poet, is
far better known than Edward III, who ruled for half of that
century. William Shakespeare outshines even Queen Elizabeth I,
whose lengthy sixteenth-century reign made hers the name later
given to the age in which Shakespeare lived and worked.

Closer to home, Langston Hughes is far better known and
infinitely more popular than Warren Harding, who was
President of the United States when Langston reached the age of
majority, or Calvin Coolidge, who was President when Langston
attended and graduated from Lincoln. Poets have a way of
outlasting politicians.

For my generation, it seems that Langston has been with
us always. We grew up reading his "Simple" columns in the
Pittsburgh Courier or one of the other Negro papers that were
sold in most parts of the country. In the all-black high schools
that we attended in the South, we memorized and recited Langston's poems in our classes and in our assemblies. I wouldn't say
we considered him a hero. He was just considered a great poet

and a great writer like the other literary figures we read in high school: people like Walt Whitman, Edgar Allan Poe, Rudyard Kipling, and Robert Frost. We took it for granted that Langston stood shoulder to shoulder with the rest.

In retrospect, I suppose that is one of the important things about our education in the segregated South. When we studied blacks or learned about "the contributions of the Negro," there were no subtle messages that these accomplishments were somehow diminished because of the color of the men and women who made them. On the contrary, if anything, they were enhanced by it.

I must confess that I did not remember that Langston Hughes graduated from Lincoln University until I started to read about the University when I was a candidate for the presidency. I probably had read somewhere before that he had gone to Lincoln. After all, I had helped K.A.B. "Soas" Jones-Quartey, a Lincoln graduate, type and proof his biography of Azikiwe (Langston's contemporary) when Jones-Quartey and I were both fellows of the Committee for the Comparative Study of New Nations at the University of Chicago in 1963–1964.

But I hadn't remembered a reference to Langston. It was a thrill, therefore, to learn six years ago that I would head the institution that counted this great poet, this giant of American letters, among its alumni.

When I was told that an anthem had been commissioned for my inauguration, and I was asked to choose the poem that would be set to music, I immediately started rereading Langston Hughes to find the appropriate text. In 1987, I chose "I Dream a World," which was set to music by Dr. John Dangerfield Cooper, a Lincoln graduate of the Class of 1947.

At the time, I did not know that the poem was actually an aria that Langston had composed for the opera *Troubled Island,* which he wrote with William Grant Still. I am not sure that Dr. John Dangerfield Cooper knew that either. I would have to learn this from Volume II of Arnold Rampersad's biography of Langston, published in 1988. You can imagine how pleased I was to see that the poem I had chosen for my inaugural anthem was the same one Dr. Rampersad used for the title of Volume II of his prize-winning biography.

I would have another connection with this wishful and wistful lyric by Langston Hughes when, in 1989, I was included in Brian Lanker's book entitled *I Dream A World: Portraits of Black Women Who Changed America.*

Finally, I should mention that one of my closest connections to Langston Hughes came through the late George Houston Bass, a dear friend of mine from Fisk, who was Langston's secretary from 1959 to 1964. As the executor of Langston's estate, and one of the guardians of Langston's literary legacy, he would have added so much to this conference today. We know that both he and Langston are smiling on us.

I started by asking how I, as President of Lincoln University, can say enough in praise of Langston Hughes. Obviously, whatever I say would not be sufficient to repay this illustrious Son of Lincoln for what he has given us as a university, us as a people, us as world. For all that he gave, we can only say an eternal "thank you."

Let this conference, which is our great celebration of the life and work of Langston Hughes, begin.

An Introduction to Arnold Rampersad

Thomas C. Phelps

National Endowment for the Humanities

Let me begin with congratulations to Emery Wimbish, Jr., and to Lincoln University for all of their hard work to put this fine conference together and to bring it to all of those who have chosen to participate in it!

Arnold Rampersad—educator, fellow, author, biographer, scholar, Woodrow Wilson Professor of Literature, and Director, Program in American Studies, Princeton University in Princeton, New Jersey.

For years he fastidiously researched the life of Langston Hughes and published the results in two volumes: *The Life of Langston Hughes, 1902–1941: I, Too, Sing America* and its companion volume, *The Life of Langston Hughes, 1941–1967: I Dream a World.* Critics abound in their acclaim for the volumes, and many named them the definitive biography of the leading poet of the Harlem Renaissance, "written," as the jacket says, "with characteristic grace and meticulous attention to detail." They are a set of books that offers "a matchless panorama of life and culture in America and abroad during the first seventy years of this century"—"a clear-eyed portrait of one of America's most controversial writers that also manages to be a sweeping depiction of the black experience in this country and abroad during the first four decades of the 20th century." No wonder the author, Arnold Rampersad, was sought after by many universities as Director of American Studies and teacher of literature. The review of *The*

Life of Langston Hughes, Volume I: 1902–1941, in *Kirkus* also praises
Dr. Rampersad for not shying from the ambiguities and ironies
in Hughes's life—"his possible homosexuality, his refusal to acknowledge the injustices in the Soviet Union while accepting
'capitalist's' donations while yet espousing the socialist cause."
Rampersad, I noticed as I read *The Life of Langston Hughes*, refuses to "beautify" his subject; instead, he evenhandedly por-
trays the whole Hughes. Successes and failures in both his life
and work are analyzed with equal care; and that is true scholarship.

     Yet Langston Hughes is not Arnold Rampersad's only sub-
ject. Indeed, he has tackled other subjects and published other
works that sparkingly display the same scholarly facets; they are
truly gems! The first cited is about Melville's *Israel Porter*, published in 1969 by Bowling Green University's Press; another, *The
Art and Imagination of W.E.B. Du Bois*, published by Harvard
University Press in 1976. With Deborah McDowell, Dr. Rampersad edited a searching examination published by Johns Hopkins
in 1989, titled *Slavery and the Literary Imagination*. Finally, he
edited a work in two volumes that I know something about because it was published by the Library of America in 1991, and
the Library of America is supported in part by grants from the
National Endowment for the Humanities—*Richard Wright:
Works*, and what a wonderful edition to the many fine works in
the Library of America collection.

     If books are not enough, Dr. Rampersad has written essays
and reviews for *Southern Review*, the *New Republic*, the *Yale Review*, and many other journals. If writing isn't enough, Dr. Rampersad has also received major fellowships from the Rockefeller
Foundation, the Guggenheim, the MacArthur Foundation, and
from the National Endowment for the Humanities. Moreover, he
serves as an adviser or on the boards of *Callaloo*, *Obsidian II*, the
Stanford Humanities Center, the Library of America, the Center
for American Culture, and *Transition*.

     It gives me great pleasure to have been asked to introduce
to you, Dr. Arnold Rampersad—educator, fellow, author, biographer, and renown scholar. Dr. Rampersad!

Langston Hughes:
The Man, the Writer, and His Continuing Influence

Arnold Rampersad
Princeton University

Thank you very much, Dr. Phelps, for your generous introduction, and thank you, also, Dr. Sudarkasa, for your wonderful introduction to the entire proceedings today. I am glad to hear the nice things that you, Dr. Phelps, have said about me, and I must reflect that although praise sometimes makes me cringe in embarrassment, the absence of praise when I am introduced makes me mad. You remained judiciously balanced between praise and calm judgment.

I am delighted to be here. Lincoln University in Pennsylvania is almost hallowed ground, as far as I am concerned, and for at least two or three reasons. It is hallowed ground because Langston Hughes went to school here, between 1926 and 1929. It is hallowed ground because I spent some important days here during my work on the project that remains the center of my career, such as it is, as a scholar of literature: my two-volume biography of Langston Hughes. The time I spent here did not add up to very much in terms of number of weeks or months, but it was crucial to my understanding of Hughes and to my sense of the importance of my project. And so I am really very delighted to be here at Lincoln again.

I also remember being here at a conference on Langston Hughes many years ago when I was starting out on that biographical enterprise, not knowing at all what I was about or what lay in store for me. I remember sitting in the back of this remarkable hall and listening to the principal speakers talk about Langston Hughes, his importance and what he had meant to some of them personally, because some of them had known him personally. I remember meeting the librarian, Professor Emery Wimbish Jr. at that time, and how subsequently he was of such enormous assistance to me, as he has been to other scholars of Langston Hughes. So I am glad that he is here today and that his name has already been mentioned in terms of his contribution to the life of the university and to the legacy of Langston Hughes in particular. I am also delighted to see another familiar face from my past research at Lincoln University, Sophy Cornwell. She, too, was of enormous assistance to me as I tried to understand Hughes's years at Lincoln, to go through the books and other material pertaining to his entire life and career that he left to Lincoln.

I am also glad to see the students here. With every visit, the faces, of course, change; but the spirit of the students does not seem to change, and I can't help but connect the spirit and the faces of the students here today with the students who were here in Langston's time—even though he was here sixty years or so ago and so much history has passed and so many profound changes have overcome our society. Still, the students here remind us not only of what Langston Hughes stood for and aimed for in his life and his art as a writer but what all the writing and publishing and teaching are about in the final analysis: the preparation and guiding of young men and women for and into the future. Langston Hughes was dedicated to helping and guiding young people, and no one would be happier than he at the presence of the students here at a conference in his name and in his honor at Lincoln University.

I am also happy to be here because I am once again in the company of my peers, my fellow scholars, my fellow toilers in the vineyard of African American literary studies—what I sometimes call the "lower forty"—those of us who, facing the vast fields of literature, are committed to draining the swamps and putting in a new crop where little or nothing was supposed to be able to grow. As I look into the audience, I see some familiar

faces, such as those of Professor Sandra Govan and Akiba Sullivan Harper. I see Jim Trotman and Bruce Kellner, David Lever-
ing Lewis, and Steve Tracy. To me, these and the others who will
come to this conference are a band of brothers and sisters to
which I am proud to belong by virtue of the kind of work we
do—part of the essential business of trying to interpret the history, the culture, the breadth, the life of Afro-America, the
African American community, as well as America in general and
even the world as seen from the African American perspective.

"Langston Hughes: The Man, the Writer, and His Continuing Influence" is supposed to be my topic today. All three factors
are of course totally, completely intertwined. Langston Hughes
liked to say, when he spoke and read his work in public (when
he gave one of the thousands of readings that were a central
feature of his life and career) that "life makes poetry." By that he
meant that life makes literature, that literature is not something
that exists apart from life, as in an ivory tower. His entire body
of work addressed not only his own generation, but also the past
and also the future generations of African Americans, certainly.

What were the characteristics of Langston Hughes's life? I
would like the freedom to sketch them out in no particular order,
certainly no order of importance. I would say that one characteristic was his utter and complete dedication to the major purpose
of his life, to the goal he loosely set himself around the age of
twenty or twenty-one, and then consolidated in the years that
immediately followed. That goal was to live by his pen, by his
writings, and by nothing else, as far as possible; and to do so—
the two aspects can't be separated—by writing mainly about
African Americans. For taking on this life, Hughes saw his father
turn his back on him after the two men struggled over Hughes's
desire to be a writer and to write about his fellow black Americans. Langston Hughes, however, accepted that rejection by his
father. He proceeded with his determination in the face of his father's disapproval with such great resolve that between his ar-
rival in New York in 1921, at the age of nineteen, to attend
Columbia University, and his death in 1967, at the age of sixty-
five, Hughes indeed lived only by writings. There were short-
lived jobs to keep him from starving in his early twenties, and
for three months each time he was twice a visiting teacher or

professor (in 1947 at Atlanta University and in 1949 at the Laboratory School of the University of Chicago). Apart from these episodes, he would allow little or nothing to deflect him from the great enterprise of his life, the great goal of writing and celebrating black life and protesting against racial injustice, that he set for himself early on.

I think of toughness as being a major characteristic of the life of Langston Hughes. His life was hard, and he certainly knew poverty at firsthand; he knew sadness and sorrow and humiliation at the hands of people with far more power and money than he had and little respect for writers, especially poets. He was in his forties before he could boast of having a thousand dollars in the bank, and he accumulated that amount only because he was on the road on one of his speaking tours and the checks were piling up in New York before he had the opportunity to use them to pay off the many debts he had incurred in the service of his craft, or incurred simply to help other people. Through all this poverty and hurt, Hughes kept on a steady keel. He was a gentle man, a soft man in many ways, sympathetic and affectionate; but he was tough to the core. One would have to be tough indeed to accomplish what Hughes accomplished despite the obstacles and hardships that he faced relentlessly.

On the other hand, Hughes was, as I have said, also tender. He was a man who loved other people and was beloved. In all my years of research on his life, it was very, very hard to find anyone who had known him who would say a harsh thing about him. It was not a question of *De mortuis nil nisi bonum* (Speak no ill of the dead). The truth is that people who knew him could remember little that wasn't pleasant. Evidently, he radiated joy and humanity, and this was how he was remembered after his death.

Paradoxically, Hughes was both a lonely and a gregarious man. He himself said, in one way or another, at one time or another, that he was essentially a lonely person, the legacy perhaps of neglect by his parents when he was a small child. On the other hand, he loved the company of people. He once quipped that he absolutely preferred to live in the city than the country because he much preferred wild people to wild animals. He needed to have people around him, and I think he needed them to counter the essential loneliness instilled in his soul from early in his life and out of which he made his literary art.

Hughes was a man of great generosity. He was generous to the young and the poor, the needy; he was generous even to his rivals. One might say that he was generous to a fault, giving to those who did not always deserve his kindness. But he was prepared to risk ingratitude in order to help younger artists in particular and young people in general.

Hughes was a man of laughter, although his laughter almost always came in the presence of tears, or the threat of tears. His first novel was *Not Without Laughter*, and a collection of stories was called *Laughing to Keep from Crying*. I think that this was essentially how he believed we must face life—with the knowledge of its inescapable loneliness and pain but with an awareness, too, of the therapy of laughter, by which we assert the human in the face of circumstances, to paraphrase Ralph Ellison. We must reach out to other people, he believed. One should not have an ascetic tolerance of life's sufferings but exuberantly explore the happy aspect of life.

What were the defining characteristics of his life as a writer? I would stress again his dedication to his craft, at two levels in particular. One might be called his dedication in general, the drive that kept him going as a poet in his early twenties when he was living from hand to mouth, working as a delivery boy for a florist, or on a vegetable farm, or on a ship up the Hudson River. All the while Hughes was writing, and not only writing but seeking publication, managing his career before he even had one, so to speak. He went down the coast of West Africa, and he worked in a Paris nightclub and wandered off to Italy, but still the writing continued and the publishing continued. And black Americans in New York, reading the *Crisis*, edited by W.E.B. Du Bois, recognized slowly but steadily that a new voice was speaking, a new poetic presence was in their midst; and they began to take Langston Hughes to their heart.

That is one level of dedication to his craft. The other has to do with the dedication he brought to each new work of art. It is often thought, and Hughes often encouraged the notion, that he almost never revised his work. Many romantic poets like to give that impression—that they never revise, that poetry is a "spontaneous overflow of emotion," to invoke Wordsworth, without mentioning that the emotion typically is "recollected in tranquility," again to quote Wordsworth. However, like Walt Whitman, Hughes's great poetic forefather in American poetry in many respects, Hughes did believe in the poetry of emotion, in the power of ideas and feelings that went beyond matters of technical craft. Hughes never wanted to be a writer who carefully sculpted rhymes and stanzas and in so doing lost the emotional heart of what he had set out to say.

Another characteristic of his writing is his versatility. By the time he was twenty-one, he had published literally in four areas: fiction, poetry, drama (a little play), and the essay. And that was the way he conceived of himself throughout his career, as someone who was an artist in words, who would venture into every single area of literary creativity because there were readers for whom a story meant more than a poem or a song lyric meant more than a story, and Hughes wanted to reach that individual and his kind. He saw himself as a poet above all, I would insist; but he wrote and staged a dozen plays, so that if he had never written a poem, he would still have a significant place in African American literature. He published dozens of short stories; about a dozen books for children; a history of the NAACP; two volumes of autobiography, *The Big Sea* and *I Wonder as I Wander;* opera libretti, song lyrics, and the like. Hughes understood, for example, that there is no writing more important than writing for children. He wrote everything. He had a sheer confidence in his versatility and in the power of his craft. Hughes has an overriding sense of social and cultural purpose tied to his sense of the past, the present, and the future of black America. I remember being told by Mrs. Cornwell to take a chance and see if the Registrar's Office might have a record of Hughes's application to Lincoln. In literally a few seconds I had it from Mrs. Bryant there.

On October 20, 1925, Hughes wrote from 1749 S. Street, NW, Washington, D.C., where he lived with his mother, to an official of Lincoln University:

> I wish to become a student at Lincoln University. I am a
> graduate of Central High School, Cleveland, Ohio, and I
> have been for one year at Columbia College in New York

City. I was forced to leave Columbia for lack of funds. But since then I have worked my way to Africa, have spent several months in Paris and three months in Italy, and on the vessel in which I earned my passage home I visited many of the Mediterranean ports. I have also spent some time in Mexico, where after my high school graduation I taught English. I have a fair knowledge of French and Spanish. My high school record admitted me to Columbia University without my taking the entrance examinations. Some of my offices and honors in high school are as follows: member of the student council, president of the American Civics Association, secretary of the French club, First Lieutenant Cadet Corp, a letter for work on the track team, and in my senior year class poet and editor of the yearbook. For some time I have been writing poetry. Many of my verses have appeared in the *Crisis and Opportunity*, *The Survey Graphic*, *The Forum*, *The World Tomorrow*, *Vanity Fair*, *The Messenger*, and *The Worker's Monthly*, as well as a number of newspapers have also published my poems. Some of them have been copied by papers in Berlin, London and Paris. A poem of mine, *The Weary Blues*, received first prize in the recent *Opportunity* contest and in the Amy Spingarn contest conducted by *The Crisis*, my essay received second prize. Early in the new year Alfred A. Knopf will publish my first book of poems. [My first book of poems, he confidently expected there to be a second, clearly.] I want to come to Lincoln because I believe it to be a school of high ideals and a place where one can study and live simply. I hope I shall be admitted. Since I shall have to depend largely on my own efforts to put myself through college if it be possible for me to procure any work at the school I would be deeply grateful to you. And because I have lost so much time, I would like to enter in February if students are admitted then. I have had no Latin, but I would be willing to remove the condition as soon as possible. I *must* go to college in order to be of more use to my race and America. I hope to teach in the South and to widen my literary activities to the field of the short story and the novel. I hope I shall hear from you soon.

Yours very sincerely,
Langston Hughes

To me this is a fascinating document. I guess that all of us have written a letter of this type at least once; some of us have done so several times, no doubt. What fascinates me first is what he has left out. There is no mention of Joplin, where he was born; or Lawrence, Kansas, where he grew up; or Lincoln, Illinois, where he wrote his first poem in the eighth grade. There is no mention of his mother and father or of his maternal grandmother, with whom he grew up as a child in Lawrence—Mary Langston, a proud and lonely woman, who told him tales, he later recalled, of heroism from the days before the Civil War and during the war and immediately after it. Surely, she told him about John Brown. The connection between Langston Hughes and Mary Langston and the figure of John Brown and the raid on Harpers Ferry is profound. As some of you know, Mary Langston's first husband, Sheridan Leary, died at Harpers Ferry fighting in John Brown's band. Mary Langston had not known what her husband was about until someone rode up to her door to tell her that he was dead and to give her his bullet-ridden shawl. This shawl she would sometimes draw over the child Langston Hughes on chilly nights in Lawrence, Kansas, when they lived together.

In this way and other ways, I am sure, she instilled in Hughes a certainty that he must make something of his life, that he could not allow himself to slip into a bourgeois fate but that he had to make a contribution not unlike that of Sheridan Leary and John Brown himself—give his life, in a way, to the cause of freedom and social justice. She herself, after the death of Leary, married another brave young abolitionist, Charles Langston, the father of Langston's mother.

Hughes wrote, "I have been for one year at Columbia College in New York." He does not mention his bitter struggle with his father, a man of some means in Mexico, over two fundamental questions. Why, his father asked, would an African American stay in America when he or she could leave? And why would anyone want to write about being an African American, when blacks were despised and mistreated? Or, as his father put it, "be a nigger among niggers"? And Langston Hughes replied, more or less: "I love them. That is where I want to be, and that is where I will stay." And that was the choice Langston made—and was making even as he applied to Lincoln University.

In writing to Lincoln about his months in Paris, Langston did not say that he washed dishes in a nightclub for a living, or that he heard wonderful American jazz music there, and wrote innovative poems that reflected those jazz rhythms. Very soon he was writing poems such as no American had ever written, in volumes such as *The Weary Blues* (1926) and *Fine Clothes to the Jew* (1927). He wrote about spending some months in Italy, but he does not write about being stranded in Genoa after having his passport and wallet stolen and watching ship after ship refuse to take him because the crew would not serve with a black man in any capacity. And Hughes sat down in, of all places, a town park named after Christopher Columbus, and wrote "I, Too" ("I, too, sing America./I am the darker brother") and sent it off to New York to raise money for the trip home.

In writing of having a fair knowledge of Spanish and French, Hughes gives a glimpse of a major feature of his life— how he would reach out to other cultures in the Caribbean, Mexico, South America, Spain, and elsewhere to try to bring their art to the attention of North American readers, so that he would eventually publish his book-length translations of the poetry of Nicolas Guillen of Cuba, Gabriela Mistral of Chile, Jacques Roumain of Haiti, and Federico García Lorca of Spain. He mentions going to Africa, but not that doing so in 1923 put him in advance of people like W.E.B. Du Bois, despite the latter's Pan-African activities. Hughes believed in doing, in travel; he used to say that if you want something bad enough, it will happen; and one important lesson of his life is that he did not stand on ceremony. He did not need to travel first-class. To see the world, he was prepared to work as a galley-slave.

The list of offices he held in high school tells us the extent to which Hughes lived both as a rebel and a pioneer, on the one hand, and in the world about him, on the other. At school he did not sulk in a corner out of self-pity or racial romanticism but put himself into a variety of situations at Central High—and all to his profit. He was broadening his knowledge of the world, deepening the foundation of his art. Hughes, the most racially committed of the major African American poets, was probably also one of the most cosmopolitan from the start to the end of his life.

In writing about *The Weary Blues*, Hughes did not discuss how it reflected a primary belief on his part: the importance of black music to any understanding of black American culture. This was his great technical discovery or commitment as a writer. By 1927, he had moved past the mere incorporation of the blues into his verse to writing blues themselves, recognizing and honoring the form as poetry. He stayed close to black music for the rest of his life—close to be-bop in the 1940s, more progressive forms of jazz still later on, and gospel music in many of his musical plays late in his life. That connection was, I think, essential to his life and to our understanding of the man, his accomplishments, and his continuing influence.

From the start of his publishing in the *Crisis* magazine, Hughes had shown his determination to experiment as a poet and not slavishly follow the tyranny of tight stanzaic forms and exact rhyme. He seemed to prefer, as had Walt Whitman and Carl Sandburg before him, to write verse that captured the realities of American speech, rather than "poetic diction," and with his ear especially attuned to the varieties of black American speech. This last aspect was a token of his emotional and esthetic involvement in black American culture, which he took as his prime source of inspiration. African Americans were "My people," as one of his early poems proclaims. His first book, *The Weary Blues*, combines these various elements: the common speech of ordinary people, jazz and blues music, and the traditional forms of poetry adapted to the African American and American subjects. The volume was unprecedented in American poetry in this blending of black and white rhythms and forms.

One cannot talk definitively about Langston Hughes the man, his work, and continuing influence without referring to his 1926 essay "The Negro Artist and the Racial Mountain," which was virtually a cultural manifesto for many of the younger writers of the Harlem Renaissance. In it, Hughes declared:

> We younger Negro artists . . . intend to express our individual dark-skinned selves without fear or shame. If white people are pleased we are glad. If they are not, it doesn't matter. We know we are beautiful. And ugly too.

> The tom-tom cries and the tom-tom laughs. If colored people are pleased we are glad. If they are not, their displeasure doesn't matter either. We build our temples for tomorrow, strong as we know how, and we stand on top of the mountain, free within ourselves.

In talking thus far about Hughes the man and his work I have not mentioned such major crises of his life as his break around 1930 with his major patron of the 1920s, Mrs. Charlotte Mason, or "Godmother," as she liked to be called; or with Zora Neale Hurston, another beneficiary of Mrs. Mason's largesse, a short time later. Nor have I mentioned Hughes's turn to the radical left in the wake of these episodes of disillusionment. From being a poet of blues and jazz he turned toward being a radical socialist poet, as in works such as "Good Morning Revolution" and "Goodbye Christ," as well as *Scottsboro Limited*, about the infamous Scottsboro case, and *Don't You Want to be Free?*, Hughes's radical play with the Harlem Suitcase Theater in 1938.

However, Hughes was not solely a radical poet during this time. In various plays, including *Mullatto* on Broadway in 1935 and other works staged by the Karamu Theater in Cleveland, Hughes emphasized the ways of racism or wrote comedies of African American life. In any event, his radical socialist phase more or less ended around 1940, when he returned, as he himself mordantly put it, to "Negroes, Nature, and Love." The entry by the United States into World War II had much to do with this turn in his career. In his autobiography *The Big Sea* (1940), his radical involvements are not mentioned at all, as Hughes pursued what might be called a centrist course even as he stepped up his attacks on segregation and Jim Crow laws in the South and elsewhere. His pamphlet of poems *Jim Crow's Last Stand*, published in 1943, epitomizes this renewed fervor. The body of work anticipates the U.S. Supreme Court decision of 1954 that marked an end to legal segregation in education and, eventually, everywhere. Hughes was always alert to what was happening in the African American world and what was coming. His volume of verse *Montage of a Dream Deferred* (1951) reflected the new and relatively new be-bop jazz rhythms that emphasized dissonance and in so doing reflected also the new pressures that were straining the black communities in the cities of the North. The best-known poem there is probably "Harlem" ("What happens to a dream deferred?").

The year 1953 was particularly important for Hughes in that it saw a major public crisis, his appearance before Senator Joe McCarthy's infamous committee on "Un-American Activities." Some observers were disappointed by Hughes's refusal to confront McCarthy, but he himself was glad to be freed at last to consolidate his position in the African American world. In the 1950s Hughes's career exploded in all directions, with his dozen or so children's books, his second autobiography, various plays, collections of his "Simple" pieces (the adventures of a Harlem character as developed in Hughes's weekly newspaper column), collections of short stories, and a large quantity of writing to be set to music in both the classical and the popular areas.

Hughes deserved this relative freedom, even if he found himself generally unable to participate personally in the latest phase of the movement for civil rights for blacks in the United States. He had been there before. He found it hard to support the exclusionary policies of the Black Power Movement, the emphasis in some quarters on hatred and violence. In March 1966, about a year before his death, he flew from his home in Harlem, New York, to Dakar in Senegal to attend the first World Festival of Negro Arts, which attracted over 2,000 delegates from around the world. Hughes stood out among all those who had come, as the poet-president of Senegal, Léopold Sédar Senghor, attested in hailing Langston Hughes as a grand figure in the evolution of black art in this century.

A *New York Times* reporter wrote home marveling about how "young writers from all over Africa followed [Hughes] about the city and haunted his hotel the way American youngsters favored baseball players." This reception was doubtless gratifying to Hughes because he craved nothing more than the admiration and affection of the peoples of African descent and because throughout his life he had been buffeted by more than his share of criticism and other attacks because of this craving. His 1927 volume of verse *Fine Clothes to the Jew*, which was saturated in the culture of the blues, probably received a more hostile reception than any book of verse by any American had ever received, with the exception of *Leaves of Grass* by Walt Whitman.

Much has happened since then, since Hughes's death the following year, in 1967. It is a good question for this conference to ask the question about Hughes's continuing influence. Should we continue to read his work, much less revere it? That question is, in effect, asked and answered every time you go by a bookstore or library or a shelf of books and you see a work by Langston Hughes. Do you take it down and read it, or do you dismiss it as *passé*, of another time? Is Hughes of another time, or is he forever? I think the majority of people in this room, by our presence here, believe that he is for the ages. Hughes undoubtedly published too much at times, and he called himself rather wearily during one period of his life "a literary sharecropper." But I think he achieved a great deal in his lifetime and has much to teach us as we move into the future.

At the end of his life, he was proud to be (according to his reckoning) the only major African American writer still living in the midst of a typical urban black community, and not in a suburb or in voluntary, comfortable exile in Turkey or Spain or some similar place. He was very proud that his life and career had been linked indissolubly with the African American world. From the start he had been responsive to the perceived needs and emotions of black Americans as well as to an inclusive view of America and the world. Much of his work celebrated the beauty and dignity and humanity of black Americans. In turn, while many writers looked elsewhere for approval and endorsement, Hughes basked in the glow of the obviously high regard of his primary audience, African Americans.

His poetry, with its original jazz and blues influences and its powerful democratic commitment, is almost certainly the most influential written by any person of African descent in this century. Certain of his poems, such as "The Negro Speaks of Rivers" or "Mother to Son," are virtual anthems of black American life and aspiration. His plays alone, as I have said, could secure him a place in Afro-American literary history. His character Simple is the most memorable single figure to emerge from black journalism. "The Negro Artist and the Racial Mountain" is timeless, it seems to me, as a statement of the constant dilemma facing the young black artist, caught between the contending forces of black and white culture and caught between class divisions within his own culture. Certainly, he was black America's most representative writer and a significant figure in world literature in the twentieth century.

Therefore, it is altogether fitting that we should be here at this conference, discussing Langston Hughes: The Man, His Works, and His Continuing Influence.

The Harlem Renaissance

Whose Sweet Angel Child?
Blues Women, Langston Hughes, and
Writing During the Harlem Renaissance

Cheryl A. Wall
Rutgers University

Reckless Blues

When I was young, nothing but a child,
When I was young, nothing but a child,
All you men tried to drive me wild.

Now I'm growing old,
Now I'm growing old,
And I got what it takes to get all you men's soul.

My mama says I'm reckless, my daddy says I'm wild,
My mama says I'm reckless, my daddy says I'm wild,
I ain't good lookin', but I'm somebody's angel child.

Daddy, Mama wants some loving; Daddy, mama wants
    some hugging
Honey, Pretty Poppa, Mama wants some loving, I vow.
Honey, Pretty Poppa, Mama wants some loving right
    now.[1]

Recorded by Bessie Smith in 1925, "Reckless Blues" is a statement of self-validation in the face of social rejection, sexual exploitation, and personal alienation. In her maturity the speaker has seized control of her sexuality—autonomy compensates for

37

aging—and relishes the pleasures that autonomy affords. The lyric dissolves the proverbial dichotomy between the good woman and the bad woman. Despite her inability to conform to the accepted standards of female beauty and her refusal to conform to the acceptable standards of female behavior, Smith's persona insists that she is *somebody's* angel child.

Smith's two accompanists on the record are Fred Longshaw, who gets composer credit for this version of a folk blues, and Louis Armstrong. Longshaw plays the harmonium; its organlike timbre complements the poignancy of the lyric and Smith's mournful contralto. But Armstrong's cornet provides the emotional counterpoint. His response to Bessie's call confirms that life's challenges can be and have been met. The last verse particularizes Smith's version of the song; it makes the point explicitly that while a woman's sexuality makes her vulnerable to male exploitation, it is the key to survival. The mood of the lyric and the music meet. Smith's increasingly assertive tone and Armstrong's increasingly intricate obbligatos culminate in the final verse to convey the persona's mastery of her life and situation. The recording documents Smith's mastery of her art.

Today, scholars recognize Bessie Smith and the so-called classic blues singers as major figures in the cultural history of the 1920s and 1930s.[2] For many writers, particularly black women writers, the blues woman is a symbol of black female creativity and autonomy whose art informs and empowers their own. That was surely not true in the blues women's time. Generally even those black intellectuals who, like W.E.B. Du Bois and Alain Locke, wrote of the profound beauty and meaning of the spirituals, were deaf to the same qualities in the blues. Blues women were even less likely than their male counterparts to have their music acknowledged as art. (Sterling Brown's poetic portrait of Ma Rainey is the most notable exception.) Among other reasons, their propensity for flamboyant dress and reckless behavior dismayed and embarrassed their more decorous brothers and sisters.

Langston Hughes was, characteristically, prescient in his understanding of the blues women's significance. As one imperative of his artistic manifesto, "The Negro Artist and the Racial Mountain," declared: "Let the blare of Negro jazz bands and the bellowing voice of Bessie Smith singing Blues penetrate the closed ears of the colored near-intellectuals until they listen and perhaps understand" (309). Not only was Hughes drawn to the compressed poetry of the blues, he aspired to a cultural role analogous to the blues troubadour. Fittingly, he was a student and admirer of the blues woman's art.

In 1926 Hughes made his pilgrimage to the Empress's domain. Bessie Smith was appearing at the Regent Theater in Baltimore when the author of the just published *The Weary Blues* made his way backstage to pay his respects. Doubtless he knew her recording "Mama's Got the Blues," which began "Some people say the weary blues ain't bad." Perhaps he hoped for recognition as a fellow blues artist. According to Hughes's biographer, Arnold Rampersad, whatever such aspirations he held were dashed. Miss Smith was not impressed. Hughes was disappointed in turn when he asked whether she had a theory about blues as Art: "Naw, she didn't know nothing about no art. All she knew was that blues had put her 'in de money'" (Rampersad, 123).

Whether she chose to theorize about it or not, Hughes understood that Bessie Smith knew a great deal about art. He understood as well that her life, and the lives of the other blues queens, could be the stuff of fiction. In his 1930 novel, *Not Without Laughter*, Hughes became the first writer to represent the figure of the blues woman in literature. His character Harriett Williams should be considered a precursor to the memorable blues women invented by Alice Walker in *The Color Purple*, Toni Cade Bambara in "Medley," and Sherley Anne Williams in *Someone Sweet Angel Child*. I want to analyze Hughes's representation and to speculate briefly about the reasons no comparable representation would appear in the fiction of black women for decades to come.

Hughes knew the folk blues from childhood. As an adult, he came to admire the so-called "classic blues" as well. Scholar Steven Tracy, whose authoritative study, *Langston Hughes & the Blues*, reconstructs the blues influences which shape and inform Hughes's poetry, notes the writer's "preference for the city, and especially vaudeville blues singers." Bessie, Mamie, Clara, and

Trixie Smith, along with Ma Rainey, were among his personal favorites (Tracy, 117–119).

Their interest in the blues was something Hughes and Carl Van Vechten (novelist, music critic, and bon vivant) shared. Hughes offered his assistance to Van Vechten when the latter wrote several pioneering articles on the blues, particularly women's blues, for the magazine *Vanity Fair*. Van Vechten was persuaded that the blues were at least equal to the spirituals as music and superior to them as poetry. Blues were "eloquent with rich idioms, metaphoric phrases, and striking word combinations" (Kellner, 44). To support his premise, Van Vechten quoted "Gulf Coast Blues," as recorded by Bessie Smith, and evoked the authority of "the young Negro poet, Langston Hughes," whose career he had begun to promote.

In a letter from which Van Vechten quotes at length, Hughes glossed the blues lyric and praised the vividness of its imagery.[3] Recounting his own visit to West Africa, he suggested a link between the blues ethos and African musical traditions. In the most incisive comment, Hughes drew his own contrast between the spirituals and the blues: "The blues always impressed me as being very sad, sadder even than the Spirituals, because their sadness is not softened with tears, but hardened with laughter. The absurd, incongruous laughter of a sadness without even a god to appeal to" (Kellner, 46). It is this laughter which his novel seeks to inscribe.

Two women embody the conflict between the spirituals and the blues in *Not Without Laughter*. Hager Williams and her youngest daughter Harriett are locked in a battle that is both philosophical and generational. Initially, Harriett appears to be her mother's opposite. Angry and rebellious, she refuses to accept the place society assigns her. She is highly intelligent but drops out of school after her seemingly liberal teacher and classmates fail to intervene when she is Jim-Crowed on a class trip. With each racist incident, Harriett's hatred of whites intensifies. In vain Hager urges her daughter to transcend bitterness. As an ex-slave, Hager recognizes the evil whites have done, yet she refuses to view them *as* evil. Instead, she grants whites a humanity equal to hers. She explains that whites are good as far as they can see, but when it comes to blacks, they cannot see far. Harriett is not moved.

No passage exemplifies Sterling Brown's description of the novel as "poetic realism" better than the prose poem recounting Hager Williams's forty years as a washerwoman: "Bought this house washin,' and made as many payments as Cudge [her husband] come near; an' raised ma chillen washin'; an' when Cudge taken sick an' laid on his back for mo'n a year I taken care o' him washin' . . . an' here I is with ma arms still in de tub!" (135–136).[4] Harriett, by contrast, refuses the domestic's role. Disgusted by the low pay, insults, and sexual harassment, she quits her job at a country club. There is no poetry in her catalog of the menial tasks required to earn a weekly wage of five dollars.

Most tellingly, Harriett rejects her mother's religion. Christianity is the bedrock out of which Hager derives her beliefs and behavioral codes. She is shocked to hear Harriett declare that the church has made "you old Negroes act like Salvation Army people . . . afraid to even laugh on Sundays, afraid for a girl and boy to look at one another, or for people to go to dances. Your old Jesus is white, I guess that's why! He's white and stiff and don't like niggers" (42). Harriett's words, like her music, are blasphemous to her mother, whose response to this particular outburst is to begin a fervent prayer.

A cultural rebel, Harriett enacts the role blues scholar William Barlow attributes to blues men: "They acted as proselytizers of a gospel of secularization in which the belief in freedom became associated with personal mobility—freedom of movement in this world here and now, rather than salvation later on in the next" (5). In Harriett's view, Hager's faith has no utility. It transforms neither Hager's material condition—the family remains poor and is occasionally destitute—nor her social status. Whites call on her to nurse their sick and comfort their bereaved, but they deny her even the respect a proper name and title confer. She is "Aunt" Hager. Bound by her work and religion, Hager is locked in place. Harriett's disavowal of Christianity enables her to imagine alternative sites.

Harriett's secular temple is the cabaret; the priests are jazz musicians.[5] In one of the novel's most extended scenes and through some of its most evocative language, Hughes depicts

BENBOW'S FAMOUS KANSAS CITY BAND in performance. The typography stresses the brashness of the commercial enterprise. The text experiments further with its transliteration of musical sounds ("Whaw-whaw . . . whaw-whaw-whaw"), as it represents the phases of performance from the "hip-rocking notes" of *Easy Rider* to the *Lazy River One-Step* to the urbane rhythms of *St. Louis Blues*.

Tellingly, the music that produces catharsis is the band's improvised rendition of a folk blues, a "plain old familiar blues, heart-breaking and extravagant, ma-baby's-gone-from-me blues." Like the other congregants, Harriett is transported. "It was true that men and women were dancing together, but their feet had gone down through the floor into the earth, each dancer's alone—down into the center of things" (93). They go to the point, perhaps, where one experiences the existential validation that one is, indeed, somebody's angel child.

However cleansing spiritually, in the social world of the novel, Harriett's behavior is irresponsible. Lost in the music, she has stayed out all night herself, and worse, she has kept her young nephew Sandy out all night as well. Awaiting Harriett's return, her mother sits "with the open Bible on her lap . . . and a bundle of switches on the floor at her feet" (98).

Clearly, Harriett is destined to leave home. Hughes constructs the narrative of her leave-taking out of the myths and legends that surrounded the blues queens. Gertrude Rainey left home at fourteen to join a vaudeville act; only after serving a long apprenticeship working tent shows did she emerge in the 1920s as the Mother of the Blues. Although Bessie Smith began her career as a professional in a traveling show in 1912 when she was eighteen, she had been singing for nickels and dimes in her hometown of Chattanooga since age nine. After leaving home and marrying at fifteen, Sippie Wallace returned and left home a second time to work as a maid and stage assistant to a snake dancer, Madame Dante, who performed in Phillips Reptile Show.[6] In like fashion, Harriett, unable to make peace with her mother or to make a life for herself, joins a carnival and hits the road.

Schooled by her brother-in-law Jimboy, an itinerant blues man, Harriett has already honed her art. Jimboy anticipates

Harriett's rebelliousness when he refuses to work under demeaning conditions. He is equally unwilling to be tied down by his family. His frequent and prolonged absences make the lines from "Gulf Coast Blues," an apt leitmotif for the character of his wife Annjee: "The mailman passed but he didn't leave no news/I'll tell the world he left me with those Gulf Coast blues."

Appropriately, too, the chapter that introduces Jimboy is called "Guitar"; he is less a fully formed character than an aesthetic principle. "Guitar" opens with a twelve-bar blues:

> Throw yo' arms around me, baby,
> Like de circle round de sun!
> Baby, throw yo' arms around me
> Like de circle round de sun,
> An' tell yo' pretty papa
> How you want yo' lovin' done. (46)

The lines function in the novel less as a sexual boast than as a celebration of the blues man's art. The blues, as Sterling Brown observed, represents collective yearnings and feelings, but, unlike the earlier musical forms of the work songs and spirituals, the life of the artist becomes the prototype of the collective. Harriett, as a member of the collective, can appropriate Jimboy's songs.

He teaches her the full range of the rural blues man's repertoire: traditional folk seculars and ballads, popular ragtime tunes, and the floating lines of the blues. The latter constitute the storehouse of blues lyrics which can be repeated and varied in limitless combinations. Jimboy is also Harriett's dance instructor; he teaches her the *parse me la*, the buck and wing, and the fundamentals of tap. In the novel's romantic representation, the blues man's art compensates for his marital infidelity and his dereliction of paternal responsibility. When Jimboy plays, "the singing notes of the guitar became a plaintive hum, like a breeze in the grove of palmettos; became a low moan, like the wind in a forest of live-oaks strung with long strands of hanging moss" (51). His talent is admirable both for the beauty it creates and for the generosity with which he shares it.

On one level, the novel encapsulates the history of the blues—representing its development from the folk blues Jimboy sings in the yard of Aunt Hager's home to the blues Harriett,

now Harrietta Williams, Princess of the Blues, performs on stage
at Chicago's Monogram Theater at the novel's conclusion. The
schematic design of the novel reinforces the link between the two
song forms. In one of her stage numbers, Harriett, dressed in a
blue calico apron with a bandanna handkerchief knotted about
her head, sings a blues she has learned from Jimboy. The lyrics
are traditional:

> It's a mighty blue mornin' when yo' daddy leaves yo' bed.
> I says a blue, blue mornin' when yo' daddy leaves yo'
>   bed—
> 'Cause if you lose yo' man, you'd just as well be dead!
>   (298)

It moves many in the audience, including Sandy's mother, to
tears. But neither its style nor its substance define Harriett.

While the blues women did demonstrate "a common
bond" with rural southern blacks, as scholar Daphne Harrison
affirms, the connection was highly mediated. Consider, for example, the complaint of blues queen Alberta Hunter. Hunter,
whose stage persona exemplified sophistication and glamour,
resented theater owners' requirement that black entertainers
conform to plantation stereotypes. "They wouldn't accept us
Negro girls in smart clothes," she complained. They insisted instead that black women perform "wearing bandannas, Aunt
Jemima dresses, and gingham aprons; the men wore overalls"
(Quoted in Taylor, 68). For reasons of profit and prejudice, theater owners sought to sustain the illusion of a fundamental
identity between performer and audience through costumes,
stage sets, and advertisements. They wished to increase the entertainers' appeal to a mass audience whose background was
predominantly southern and rural, and they were loath to grant
complex identities to either their employees or their customers.

Not Without Laughter highlights the shifting personas that
blues women assumed on stage and off. For her initial entrance,
Harriett is dressed in "glowing orange, flame-like against the
ebony of her skin" (297). The effect is to evoke the image of a
jungle princess and to enforce the myth of exotic primitivism
that was pervasive during the 1920s. The description of the song
she sings, "a popular version of an old Negro melody, refashioned with words from Broadway," helps the reader deconstruct

the image as commercial and counterfeit. After singing the folk blues, Harriett reappears: "Her final number was a dance-song which she sang in a sparkling dress of white sequins, ending the act with a mad collection of steps and a swift sudden whirl across the whole stage as the orchestra joined Billy's piano in a triumphant arch of jazz" (298). Its placement at the end of her performance suggests that this is the persona which embodies Harriett's greatest achievement as an artist. The triumph inheres as well in Harriett's successful invention of a life which she can lead without denying her self.

But the price is high. *Not Without Laughter* is honest enough in its depiction of Harriett's life to show her broke and stranded in Memphis—she has quit the carnival because she was not being paid—and to allude to the prostitution which she practices when she has no other way to earn a living.[7] It notes the latter by interpolating a news clipping headlined NEGRESSES ARRESTED, which both provides the information and comments on the dominant society's refusal to recognize the individual humanity of black people. In addition to countering such stereotyped racial and gender representations, the novel refuses to reinscribe the good woman/bad woman dichotomy. Indeed it subverts that dichotomy in the same way "The Reckless Blues" does. Harriett, a scarlet woman—in one of the novel's many allusions to Hughes's poetry, she wears red silk stockings—is also the guardian angel who enables Sandy to fulfill Hager's dream for him.

Harriett and Sandy are reunited when he and Annjee attend her performance. Harriett castigates her sister for requiring Sandy to quit school and take a job running an elevator. She promises to give him the money he would have earned. The words that accompany her gesture strain credulity. Harriett says to her sister that "you and me was foolish, all right, breaking mama's heart, leaving school, but Sandy can't do like us. He's gotta be what his grandma Hager wanted him to be—able to help the black race, Annjee! You hear me? Help the whole race!" (303). The gesture itself does not.

Although the story emphasizes Harriett's estrangement from her mother, the discourse of the novel inscribes a common bond. One key imagistic link is the figure "whirl."[8] It is first associated with Harriett at the moment that Sandy discovers her performing at the carnival. Then in a passage that begins by identifying Harriett, Jimboy, Hager, and Afro-Americans generally as "a band of dancers," the figure is applied to Hager. "Sandy remembered his grandmother whirling around in front of the altar at revival meetings in the midst of the other sisters, her face shining with light, arms outstretched as though all the cares of the world had been cast away" (293). Finally, at the culmination of her performance as the Princess of the Blues, Harriett performs "a swift sudden whirl across the whole stage." In each instance, whirling becomes a sign of spiritual release. Following a pattern characteristic of African religious practices, spiritual ecstasy is manifested in sudden, intense physical movement.[9] Whirling signals the momentary freedom from the oppression and sadness which define much of these characters' lives. Truly Hager's daughter, Harriett finds in Afro-American secular music the joy her mother found in the Christian God.

Hughes's representation of the blues woman invests her with moral and spiritual power. She is an artist who, despite her professional success, bespeaks the aspirations and desires of the masses. The novel draws a sharp distinction between Harriett, as the avatar of a new generation, and her snobbish sister, Tempy. Tempy mouths the rhetoric of the New Negro and reads *The Crisis*, the journal of the National Association for the Advancement of Colored People edited by Du Bois, while acting out an extreme form of racial self-hatred. By contrast, Harriett's militancy grows out of a hard-won self love, that is uncountenanced by social or divine authority. Harriett follows her own path to self validation. Yet, as a model for the women in her audience, she charts the way for others to identify themselves as "somebody's angel child."

Given the role the blues woman played in Afro-American culture during the 1920s, her total absence from the work of contemporary black women writers is striking. None of the Harlem Renaissance women writers, including Jessie Fauset, Nella Larsen, Marita Bonner, Gwendolyn Bennett, and Georgia Douglas Johnson fashioned a character after the blues queens.[10] Few of them even acknowledged the existence of the blues. The blues woman, whose penchant for wild and reckless living was well known even to those who never deigned to listen to her music, could not be embraced by her literary sisters until the impulse toward conformity, decorousness, and the staider forms of uplift was spent. Only when black women writers ceased to valorize "the careful development of thrift, patience, high morals, and good manners" to the exclusion of the "dreadful funkiness of passion, the funkiness of nature, the funkiness of the wide range of human emotions," as Toni Morrison phrases it in *The Bluest Eye* (64), was the blues woman welcomed in her sisters' fiction.

Even Zora Neale Hurston, the one literary woman who embraced the cultural legacy that was the blues and who had little patience with any kind of racial uplift, did not represent a blues woman in her prose. When, for example, in *Their Eyes Were Watching God* she sought to give her heroine Janie Crawford access to the liberating and self-affirming ethic of the blues, she invented a male character, Tea Cake, to be Janie's mentor. If she did not create a fictional blues woman—though one could argue contrarily that the character Janie is informed by the blues ethos and floating blues lines recur throughout the novel—Hurston did pay her personal homage to Bessie Smith. She met her in the company of Langston Hughes.

During the summer of 1927, Hurston and Hughes crossed paths unexpectedly in New Orleans. She was beginning her field work; he was visiting the South for the first time. When they met, he had already listened both to records and street singers in Baton Rouge and New Orleans and "heard many of the blues verses [he] used later in [his] short stories and [his] novel" (*The Big Sea*, 290). Earlier that year he had drawn on similar models to write the poems in the landmark volume, *Fine Clothes to the Jew*, his "most radical achievement in language" (Rampersad, 141). Still, despite the great bravado with which he had renounced the impulse toward propriety in "The Negro Artist and the Racial Mountain," he had limited firsthand knowledge of the lives of the "low-down" folk he celebrated. He knew that in Hurston he would have the ideal tutor to instruct him in southern black culture and folkways. "Blind guitar players, conjur (sic) men, and former slaves were her quarry, small town jooks and plantation churches, her haunts" (*The Big Sea*, 296). He expected that it would be fun traveling with Hurston, and it was.

In Macon, Georgia, they heard Bessie Smith sing in a small theater. Of course, as Hughes jested, one did not have to go near the theater to hear Bessie sing; she could be heard from blocks away. Due doubtless to the exigencies of segregation, the Empress and the two writers were staying at the same hotel. There they heard Smith practice every morning; they met and "got to know her pretty well" (296). "With Hurston taking the lead," Rampersad concludes, "Smith was warmer this time to the Bard of the Blues" (153). Hughes reciprocated the gesture in his representation of Harriett Williams, a portrait of the blues woman as artist and hero.[11] Perhaps in their shared encounter, Zora Neale Hurston helped Langston Hughes gain possession of his own sweet angel child.

NOTES

1. "Reckless Blues," Columbia 14056-D.

2. See, for example, Hazel Carby, "It Jus Be's Dat Way Sometime: The Sexual Politics of Women's Blues," and Cheryl A. Wall, "Poets and Versifiers, Singers and Signifiers: The Women of the Harlem Renaissance."

3. Clarence Williams was the composer credited with "Gulf Coast Blues," which Bessie Smith recorded on February 16, 1923 (Columbia A3844); it was the "B" side of her first Columbia Records release, "Down Hearted Blues."

4. Sterling Brown referred to the novel's "poetic realism" in his review in *Opportunity*, 8 (September 1930), and in *The Negro in American Fiction*, where he called the novel "one of the best by a Negro author" (155).

5. The representation of jazz musicians as priestly figures anticipates James Baldwin's more elaborate representation in "Sonny's Blues" and *Another Country*. So, too, does Harriett prefigure the representation of Ida Scott, the blues woman who is sister to the novel's protagonist.

6. For further biographical information, see Sandra Lieb, Mother of the Blues: A Study of Ma Rainey; Chris Albertson, Bessie; and Daphne Duval Harrison, Black Pearls: Blues Queens of the 1920s.

7. At other points, particularly in the description of life in "the Bottoms," the novel does romanticize the lives of the poor. Describing the neighborhood as "a gay place," the narrator asserts that "in the Bottoms folks ceased to struggle against the boundaries between good and bad, or white and black, and surrendered amiably to immorality" (216).

8. Hughes employed the figure most famously in the poem "Dream Variation," which begins "To fling my arms wide/In some place of the sun,/To whirl and to dance/Till the white day is done." Selected Poems (14).

9. Albert Raboteau asserts that despite the discontinuities in the tenets of belief, "it is in the context of action, the patterns of motor behavior preceding and following the ecstatic experience, that there may be a continuity between African and American forms of spirit possession" (64–65).

10. Jessie Fauset comes closest with Marise Davies, a character in Comedy: American Style (1933), whose career seems inspired by Josephine Baker's.

11. By the time Not Without Laughter was published, Hughes and Hurston were no longer friends. Thereafter, they rarely spoke about, let alone to, each other. Accounts of their friendship, artistic collaboration, and disaffection are collected in Langston Hughes and Zora Neale Hurston, Mule Bone, edited by George Houston Bass and Henry Louis Gates Jr. (New York: Harper Perennial, 1991).

WORKS CITED

Albertson, Chris. *Bessie*. New York: Stein and Day, 1972.

Barlow, William. *Looking Up at Down: The Emergence of Blues Culture.* Philadelphia: Temple University Press, 1989.

Brown, Sterling. "The Blues." *Phylon* 13 (Autumn 1952): 286–292.

———. *Negro Poetry and Drama and The Negro in American Fiction.* 1937. Rpt. New York: Atheneum, 1969.

———. Review of *Not Without Laughter. Opportunity* 8 (September 1930): 279–280.

Carby, Hazel. "It Jus Be's Dat Way Sometime: The Sexual Politics of Women's Blues." *Radical America* 20.4 (1986): 9–22.

Harrison, Daphne Duval. *Black Pearls: Blues Queens of the 1920s*. New Brunswick, NJ: Rutgers University Press, 1988.

Hughes, Langston. *The Big Sea*. 1940. Rpt. New York: Hill & Wang, 1963.

———. "The Negro Artist and the Racial Mountain." 1926. Rpt. in Nathan Huggins, ed. *Voices from the Harlem Renaissance*. New York: Oxford University Press, 1976.

———. *Not Without Laughter*. 1930. Rpt. New York: Macmillan, Collier Books Edition, 1969.

———. *Selected Poems*. 1959. New York: Vintage, 1974.

———, and Zora Neale Hurston. *Mule Bone*. Edited with Introductions by George Houston Bass and Henry Louis Gates, Jr. New York: Harper Perennial, 1991.

Kellner, Bruce, ed. *Keep a Inchin' Along: Selected Writings of Carl Van Vechten about Black Art and Letters*. Westport, CT: Greenwood Press, 1979.

Lieb, Sandra. *Mother of the Blues: A Study of Ma Rainey*. Amherst: University of Massachusetts Press, 1981.

Morrison, Toni. *The Bluest Eye*. New York: Holt, Rinehart and Winston, 1970.

Raboteau, Albert. *Slave Religion*. New York: Oxford University Press, 1978.

Rampersad, Arnold. *The Life of Langston Hughes: Vol. I: I, Too, Sing America*. New York: Oxford University Press, 1986.

Taylor, Frank. *Alberta Hunter: A Celebration in Blues*. New York: McGraw-Hill, 1987.

Tracy, Steven C. *Langston Hughes & the Blues*. Urbana: University of Illinois Press, 1988.

Wall, Cheryl A. "Poets and Versifiers, Singers and Signifiers: the Women of the Harlem Renaissance." Virginia Lussier and Kenneth Wheeler, eds. *Women, the Arts, and the 1920s in Paris and New York*. New Brunswick, NJ: Transaction Books, 1982.

Langston Hughes:
Poetry, Blues, and Gospel—Somewhere to Stand

Steven C. Tracy

The Greek mathematician and inventor Archimedes once said, "Give me somewhere to stand and I will move the earth." Literary artists, too, must find their places to stand in order to move the earth. And certainly the best of them plant their feet where the ground seems to them to be most stable, especially when their mission is to move the firmament from the shoulders of Atlas onto their own, to provide some new, revolutionary, and mountainous foundation for our visionary dreams. In the midst of that Modernist revolution we know as the Harlem Renaissance or the New Negro Movement, there was a figure who sought to change the way we looked not only at art and African Americans, but also at the world. His vision was modernistic: experimental, both spontaneous and improvisatory and thoughtfully and carefully crafted, at times primitivistic, disjunctive, and cacophonous, rejecting artificial middle-class values, promoting emotional and intellectual freedom, and, above all, life- and love-affirming—self-affirming. And not only affirming of the African American self, though certainly Langston Hughes spent a lifetime climbing the racial mountain and living and affirming an African American self, but also affirming what Ralph Ellison called in *Invisible Man* the principle "dreamed into being out of the chaos and darkness of the feudal past" (574).

"Freedom!/Brotherhood!/ Democracy!" Hughes hallelu-
jahed in "Freedom's Plow:"

> ... for everybody,
> For all America, for all the world.
> May its branches spread and its shelter grow
> Until all races and all people know its shade.
> (*Selected Poems*, 297)

Langston Hughes planted his feet among the Warren Street Bap-
tists in Lawrence, with their "fiery sermons, inspired responses,
and passionate, skilled singing" (Rampersad, I, 16); among the
"ordinary Negroes" of Seventh Street in Washington, D.C., were
people who drew no color line, "played the blues, ate water-
melon, barbecue, and fish sandwiches, shot pool, told tall tales,
looked at the dome of the Capitol and laughed out loud"
(Hughes, *The Big Sea*, 209); among, as he called them, proudly
jubilantly, "the low-down folks":

> The so-called common element, and they are the major-
> ity—may the Lord be praised! . . . They furnish a wealth of
> colorful, distinctive material for any artist because they
> still hold their individuality in the face of American stan-
> dardizations. ("The Negro Artist," 306)

"The tom-tom of revolt against weariness in a white world"
he called jazz, referring clearly to the spectrum of African
American folk music ("The Negro Artist," 308). For his vision of
African American music—sacred and secular—was comprehen-
sively affectionate, much more so than Du Bois's, Johnson's, and
Locke's, all of whom preferred spirituals to blues and jazz, Du
Bois even terming jazz "caricature" (*Dusk of Dawn*, 202–203). But,
for Hughes, African American music was elemental, primal:

> Like the waves of the sea coming one after another, always
> one after another, like the earth moving around the sun,
> night, day—night, day—night, day—forever, so is the un-
> dertow of black music with its rhythm that never betrays
> you, its strength like the beat of the human heart, its hu-
> mor, and its rooted power. (*The Big Sea*, 209)

The beat of the heart, the pulse—Hughes used these metaphors
repeatedly in reference to the folklore of his people; and his work

from *The Weary Blues* through *The Panther and the Lash* throbbed with ethno-poetic splendor.

The fact that Hughes could throw one arm around spirituals and gospel music and the other around the blues simultaneously would seem remarkable, even blasphemous, in some circles, primarily Christian ones where the blues might be dubbed "the devil's music." But Hughes sat them rather comfortably side by side in his work and his ethos: "I liked the barrel houses of Seventh Street, the shouting churches, and the songs," he wrote in *The Big Sea* (209); the following year he called spirituals and blues the "two great Negro gifts to American music" ("Songs Called the Blues," 143). In the mid-fifties his devil figure Big Eye Buddy Lomax, in both the play and the novel *Tambourines to Glory*, asserted that "them gospel songs sound just like the blues," to which the holy sister managed only the feeble reply, "At least our words is different" (*Tambourines*, 126–27).

It is clear that Hughes did not exalt spirituals and gospel music based on any fervent belief in Christianity. The "Salvation" chapter in *The Big Sea* outlines his traumatic (non-) conversion experience that left him doubting the existence of a Jesus who had not come to help him (18–21); and his poem "Mystery" describes the feelings of an uninitiated thirteen-year-old, isolated by her confused uncertainty, yoking "The mystery/and the darkness/and the song/and me" (*Selected Poems*, 256). In "To Negro Writers" he called on his African American colleagues to "expose the sick-sweet smile of organized religion . . . and the half-voodoo, half-clown face of revivalism, dulling the mind with the clap of its empty hands" (139). His "first experience with censorship" he recounted in "My Adventures as a Social Poet," reporting how a preacher directed him not to read any more blues in his pulpit (206). Years later in a Simple story, "Gospel Singers," Simple compares churches to movie theaters, preachers to movie stars, and church services to shows during which gospel singers are "working in the vineyards of the Lord and digging in his gold mines," joking that when you hear gospel singers "crying 'I Cannot Bear My Burden Alone,' what they really mean is, 'Help me get my cross to my Cadillac.'" (*Simple's Uncle Sam*, 39). Significantly, though, Simple did not mind paying to hear the gospel singers—paying twice, even—

because he felt that "the music that these people put down can't be beat" (39). For Simple, as for Hughes, it was not the meaning of the words so much as the wording of the means that carried him away. What Hughes said about the blues in "Songs Called the Blues" applies to gospel music as well: "You don't have to understand the words to know the meaning of the blues, or to feel their sadness or to hope their hopes" (145). Paul Oliver's description of gospel music captures the essence of the spark of gospel music that ignited Hughes:

> Gospel songs bring the message of "good news" and are so called, according to some preachers, because they state the "gospel truth." The promise of a better life hereafter still pervades them but their joyousness and extrovert behavior suggest happiness achieved in this life in preparation for the next. (199)

In the melisma and glissandi of "the wordless moan, that is the essence of gospel music" (Heilbut, 23), Hughes heard the pulsing drama of the life of the spirit, the human spirit. It was a spirit he tried to capture in poems like "Fire" and "Sunday Morning Prophecy" and in gospel plays like *Tambourines to Glory*, the highly successful *Black Nativity* and *Jericho-Jim Crow*, and *The Gospel Glory*.

Hughes heard that pulse in the blues too, of course. Buddy Lomax was certainly right in hearing similarities between gospel and blues music. Robert Farris Thompson has pointed out the influence of the "Ancient African organizing principle of song and dance" on African American music as a whole, with its "dominance of a percussive performance attack. . . , propensity for multiple meter. . . , overlapping and response. . . , inner pulse control. . . , suspended accentuation pattern. . . , and songs and dances of social allusion" (xiii). It is not surprising that one of the founding fathers of gospel music, Thomas A. Dorsey, who came to religious prominence with the publication of *Gospel Pearls* in 1921 by the Sunday School Publishing Board of the National Baptist Convention, had been a blues and hokum singer. One of Dorsey's biggest hokum hits had been "It's Tight Like That" with singer-guitarist Tampa Red. Eventually, though, Dorsey went from being "tight like that" to being tight with God, penning such standards as "Precious Lord Take My Hand" and

"Peace in the Valley." It was the *manner* of performing, the spirit of the performance, that transcended the sometimes artificial sacred, secular, and profane bounds and linked black musics together.

Certainly Hughes wrote more about blues than he did about gospel music in his lifetime. He recalled the first time he heard the blues in Kansas City on the appropriately named Independence Avenue, which provided him with material for his "The Weary Blues," one of the poems, with "Jazzonia" and "Negro Dancers," that Hughes placed beside Vachel Lindsay's plate at the Wardman Park Hotel; the blues of Ma Rainey and the boogie woogie and ragtime piano players on State Street in Chicago; the blues, ragtime, and jazz of Harlem from the twenties on; aboard the S.S. *Malone* bound for Africa, even at Le Grand Duc in France:

> Blues in the Rue Pigalle. Black and laughing, heartbreaking blues in the Paris dawn, pounding like a pulse beat, moving like the Mississippi. (*The Big Sea*, 162)

The yoking of the pulse beat, the river, and the singing links this description with another of Hughes's classic poems, "The Negro Speaks of Rivers," reminding us, as Hughes wrote with Milton Meltzer in *Black Magic*, that the "syncopated beat which the captive Africans brought with them" that found its first expression here in "the hand-clapping, feet-stomping, drum-beating rhythms (related, of course, to the rhythms of the human heart)" (4–5), is as "ancient as the world." After Le Grand Duc in Washington, D.C., and collecting with Zora Neale Hurston throughout the South—"All my life," Hughes wrote, "I've heard the blues" ("I Remember the Blues," 152). He continued to admire their expressive beauty, differentiating them clearly from the spirituals as being "sadder . . . because their sadness is not softened with tears, but hardened with laughter, the absurd, incongruous laughter of sadness without a god to appeal to" (Van Vechten, 86). To him they were "sad songs sung to the most despondent rhythm in the world . . ." (review of *Blues: An Anthology*, 258), at times "as absurd as Krazy Kat" (Van Vechten, 86), but nearly always conveying "a kind of marching on syncopation, a gonna-make-it-somehow determination in spite of it all, that ever-present laughter-under-sorrow that indicates a love of life too precious to let it go" ("I Remember the Blues," 155), with "a steady rolling beat that seemed to be marching somewhere to something better, to something happy" (*First Book of Jazz*, 37). Despite the differences between spirituals and blues that Hughes enumerated in "Songs Called the Blues," he saw a greater inherent bond that transcended what he saw as the superficial discordances between the blues and spiritual and gospel music. The music, his art, black art, was not to be isolating but ultimately unifying, and if what Arnold Rampersad described as Hughes's "cloistered life" (16) with Mary Langston accentuated his solitude, the visceral drama of black music—tender, humorous, tragic, innocent, sexy, ecstatic, mundane, playful, lively and deadly serious—set the stage for his emergence as an artist.

In fact, Hughes sought to infuse much of his poetry with the urgency, the immediacy, of activity and performance. He wrote in "Aunt Sue's Stories:"

> Black slaves
> Working in the hot sun,
> And black slaves
> Walking in the dewy night,
> And black slaves
> Singing sorrow songs on the banks of a mighty river
> Mingle themselves softly
> In the flow of Aunt Sue's voice,
> Mingle themselves softly
> In the dark shadows that cross and recross
> Aunt Sue's stories. (*Selected Stories*, 6)

Hughes delighted in reciting his poetry to musical accompaniment, seeing the performance as an occasion for meaningful group interaction that would enhance and strengthen communication. Ezra Pound wrote to Hughes about a poem Hughes sent to him: "Thank God; at last I come across a poem I can understand" (Hentoff, 27). The comment is ironic coming from Pound, but perfectly appropriate in regard to Hughes's intentions and achievement. Nat Hentoff reported Hughes's designs for his recitations with musical accompaniment:

> The music should not only be a background to the poetry, but should comment on it. I tell the musicians—and I've worked with several different modern and traditional

groups—to improvise as much as they care around what I read. Whatever they bring of themselves to the poetry is welcome to me. I merely suggest the mood of each piece as a general orientation. Then I listen to what they say in their playing, and that affects my own rhythms when I read. We listen to each other. (27)

The performance of the poem, then, becomes a nexus, a dialogue, something as old as the inception of the poem but as new as the inflection of the impulse. Indeed, in the stage directions to *Tambourines to Glory* Hughes suggested that "audience participation might be encouraged—singing, foot-patting, handclapping—and in the program the lyrics of some of the songs might be printed with an invitation to sing the refrains along with the chorus of Tambourine Temple" (184). It would not likely take much to inspire participation for, as Hughes wrote in "Spirituals," "Song is a strong thing" (*Selected Poems*, 28).

Now Hughes had his limitations as a commentator on the blues. His discussions of the roots of the blues in African music and work songs and field hollers were often general and unsystematic early in his career, though his later work was somewhat more comprehensive. He overgeneralized a bit about the types of blues that males sang as opposed to females, and he did not adequately convey the breadth of themes or stanzaic patterns present in the blues. His lists of outstanding blues singers most often emphasized vaudeville blues singers, certainly urban blues singers at any rate, indicating more of a preference for sophisticated productions. Indeed, Hughes wrote that it was a desire of his to write the first libretto for a blues opera ("From the Blues to an Opera Libretto"), and he himself was ambivalent about whether he was a folk poet or a folk person, discussing the subject in equivocal terms:

I have tried to get that quality into my, shall we call them, created blues, because of course I consciously write these, and so I guess you can't call them real folk blues, unless you want to say that I'm a folk poet, myself a folk person, which maybe I am. (*Langston Hughes Reads and Talks*).

The blues poems that Hughes wrote were often thematic rather than associative, and they contained noticeably few references to drugs, sex, and violence in comparison to blues songs recorded both in the field and in the studio, opting for something of a via media in reflecting the themes and images of the folk tradition. His language and images, in fact, are not often as stark or startling as the best blues lyrics by performers within the oral tradition, but they make excellent use of both oral and written traditions in a way that adds materially to both, making his poetry something quite familiar, yet quite new.

Of course, not all of Hughes's blues poems did employ blues stanza forms. Hughes called his poem "Cross," for example, a poem whose "mood is that of the blues, although its lyric form lacks the folk repetition" ("From the Blues to an Opera Libretto"). It is not stanza form, repetition, or the number of measures in a stanza that makes the blues—but the feeling, spirit, attitude, and approach. And these, indeed, imbue much of the poetry of Langston Hughes to such an extent that the whine of a bottleneck, or the wail of a harmonica, or the trill of a piano may be regularly inferred as the subtext of his work. Behind the "Troubled Woman"

> Bowed by
> Weariness and pain
> like an
> Autumn flower
> In the frozen rain. (*Selected Poems*, 77)

or the "Island" toward which the speaker wishes to be taken by the "wave of sorrow" because of its fair sands (*Selected Poems*, 78), or the question

> Where is the Jim Crow section
> On this merry-go-round
> Mister, cause I want to ride? (*Selected Poems* 194)

or the

> Hit me! Jab Me!
> Make me say I did it. (*Selected Poems*, 197)

of "Third Degree," or the words of "The Negro Mother"

> For I will be with you till no white brother
> Dares keep down the children of the Negro Mother. . . .
> (*Selected Poems*, 289)

are the strains of black life and black song.

All of which leads us to the performance aspect of my discussion today, and the chance to hear some of those songs that seem to be patterned after recognizable stanza forms, both gospel and blues.

Most common in the tradition and in Hughes's work is the twelve-bar blues form. The first song I'm going to perform is "Early Evening Quarrel" from *Shakespeare in Harlem*, a kind of comedy blues dialogue in the tradition of such male-female recording teams as Butterbeans and Susie or Lonnie Johnson and Victoria Spivey or Clara Smith. The argument's pace and back-and-forth exchange is captured well in Hughes's strategy of giving a twelve-bar chorus each to Hattie and Hammond, where both lay out their arguments in the traditional stanza form paced in a slower fashion by using the repeat lines of the AAB stanza, and then speeding up by having the two exchange quips in one twelve-bar stanza, the lines coming at the rate of one line per bar.

The poem Hughes entitled "Death Chant" in *Shakespeare in Harlem* and "Stony Lonesome" in his *Selected Poems* is another twelve-bar blues but noticeably less urbane and more low-down than "Early Evening Quarrel." Hughes accomplishes this through bluntness and repetition in his diction and by controlling the pace with his line placement, sometimes dividing a single "line" in the AAB stanza, which he usually rendered in two lines, into three lines of four, three, or two words each. The mood of the poem is also achieved by the expletives at the end of each stanza, which violate the strict twelve-bar blues pattern and emphasize the singer's focus on the emotional content rather than the strict technical context of the performance. The original title is somewhat of a directive as to how to hear or sing the song—like a chant—and the later one describes how it should sound as well—stony lonesome.

On his Spoken Arts recording Hughes said that he wrote "Bound No'th Blues" in "the exact format of the traditional folk blues." It is another moaning blues that makes noticeable use of repetition to create pace and mood, and the theme of wandering alone in the world down some interminable road is common in blues lyrics.

One of Hughes's most successful gospel-influenced poems was "Fire." It is immediately apparent that "Fire" and such poems as "Stony Lonesome" and "Bound No'th Blues" have a great deal in common. Pace and mood are once again controlled and slowed by repetition and line placement, and the emotional force of the passage resides in the triadic refrain, which builds from one word in the first line to two in the second to an outburst of five in the third, and then becomes a refrain of five lines, the final three elongated anguished cries, at the end.

"Southern Mammy Sings" and "Same In Blues" are two poems that borrow structurally from eight-bar blues lyrics, both of which use modulated refrains that encapsulate the essence of what has come before them. In "Southern Mammy" the refrain becomes more assertive than the narrative section; in "Same In" the refrain sums up the psychological effect of the narrative section as it is related to broader social issues. In this way, Hughes modifies the oral tradition to great literary effect.

Hughes liked humor, of course, and one of his best humorous blues poems is "Morning After." His final two lines,

> You just a little bit o' woman but you
> Sound like a great big crowd

could in fact be a metaphor for African American blues and gospel: they may seem small and unimposing, but you should hear them roar.

And resound.

WORKS CITED

Du Bois, W.E.B. *Dusk of Dawn*. New York: Harcourt, Brace, 1940.

Ellison, Ralph. *Invisible Man*. New York: Vintage, 1989.

Hentoff, Nat. "Langston Hughes: He Found Poetry in the Blues." *Mayfair* (August 1958): 26, 27, 43, 45–47, 49.

Hughes, Langston. *The Big Sea*. New York: Hill & Wang, 1963.

———. In *The First Book of Jazz*. Eds. Cliff Roberts and David Martin. New York: Franklin Watts, 1976.

———. "From the Blues to an Opera Libretto." *New York Times.* January 15, 1950.

———. "I Remember the Blues." In *Missouri Reader*. Ed. Frank Luther Mott. Columbia: University of Missouri Press, 1964. 152–155.

———. "My Adventures as a Social Poet." *Phylon* 6 (1947): 205–213.

———. "The Negro Artist and the Racial Mountain." In *Voices from the Harlem Renaissance*. Ed. Nathan I. Huggins. New York: Oxford University Press, 1976. 305–309.

———. *Reads and Talks*. Spoken Arts 7140, 1959.

———. "Review of *Blues: An Anthology* by W.C. Handy." *Opportunity* (August 1926): 258.

———. *Selected Poems*. New York: Vintage Books, 1984.

———. *Simple's Uncle Sam*. New York: Hill & Wang, 1965.

———. "Songs Called the Blues." *Phylon* 2.2 (1941): 143–145.

———. *Tambourines to Glory*. New York: John Day, 1958. Novel.

———. *Tambourines to Glory*. In *Five Plays by Langston Hughes*. Bloomington: Indiana University Press, 1968.

———. "To Negro Writers." *American Writer's Congress*. Ed. Henry Hart. New York: International Publisher, 1935. 139–141.

———, and Milton Meltzer, eds. *Black Magic. A Pictorial History of the Negro in American Entertainment*. Englewood Cliffs, NJ: Prentice-Hall, 1967.

Oliver, Paul, Max Harrison, and William Bolcom. *The New Grove Gospel, Blues and Jazz, with Spirituals and Ragtime*. London: Macmillan, 1986.

Rampersad, Arnold. *The Life of Langston Hughes: Volume 1: 1902–1941: I, Too, Sing America*. New York: Oxford University Press, 1986.

Thompson, Robert Farris. *Flash of the Spirit: African and AfroAmerican Art and Philosophy*. New York: Random House, 1983.

Van Vechten, Carl. "The Black Blues." *Vanity Fair* 24.6 (1925): 57, 86, 92.

Africanisms and Postmodernist Imagination in the Popular Fiction of Langston Hughes

Ropo Sekoni
Lincoln University

The Harlem Renaissance remains one of the most discussed aspects of African American cultural productions. Writings on this fertile period in African American literary and artistic experience range from a discussion of it as an indigenous cultural revolution to an examination of the Harlem Renaissance as a special variant of a more general aesthetic experiment—modernism (Baker 1988). Since most of the writings on this phase of African American literature often focused on the elucidation of the writings of individual authors within the tradition and, more often than not, on the belletristic aspects of the works of such authors, the elaborate thematization and anticipation of most of the artistic and cultural themes of postmodernism in the writing of Harlem Renaissance authors have been overlooked by several critics. One aspect that is often glossed over by critics is the involvement of the Harlem Renaissance writers in the popularization of postmodernist imagination in some of their works. Some of such writers, aspects of whose works evoke in terms of both form and content themes of postmodernism, are Zora Neale Hurston and Langston Hughes.

Since I have examined the role of Africanisms in the postmodernist sensibility of Hurston elsewhere, this paper will investigate the strategies of thematizing postmodernist imagination in Langston Hughes's popular fiction—the stories about Jesse B. Semple.

Just as Baker and others have aptly observed that there are connections between modernism and the Harlem Renaissance aesthetic, especially in the realm of the appropriation of "primitivist" and folk cultural forms, crosscurrents between postmodernism and African philosophical and aesthetic strategies are conceivable (Baker 1984). Despite the paucity of direct philosophic discourse in African precolonial oral traditions, African cultural and artistic practices are characterized by indirect thematization of the most recurrent topic in postmodernist discourse—the crisis of representation. The appropriation and reuse of traditional African and African American cultural and aesthetic forms are capable, as will be demonstrated later, to facilitate and reinforce the thematization of postmodernism.

By way of a brief summary of the major concerns, themes, and motifs of postmodernism in art and culture, the characterizations of postmodernism as a social and aesthetic movement by Roy Boyne and Ali Rattansi (1990) are worth borrowing as specific paradigms under which Langston Hughes's exploration and manifestation of postmodernist imagination can be attempted. In a critical reading of major texts of postmodernist theory such as Lyotard's *The Postmodern Condition*, Rorty's *Pragmatism*, and Derrida's *Logocentrism*, Boyne and Rattansi attempted to identify specific characteristics of postmodernist discourse that are otherwise implicit in the writings of Lyotard in particular. Some of the features of postmodernist imagination identified by Boyne and Rattansi are (1) the crisis of representation; (2) the fragmentation of identity and the resultant privileging of pluralism and recovery of the discourse of the other; (3) the dissolution of boundaries between "high" and "mass" culture; (4) preoccupation with the merger of "art" and life; (5) an eclectic mixing of codes and styles; (6) disbelief in the power of totalising modes of knowledge and the resultant acceptance of polyvocality; and (7) a critique of dualism and binarism (Boyne and Rattansi, 9–13).

Although most of the discursive data often cited to illustrate postmodernist imagination and cultural praxis is derived from Western discursive heritage, the interconnection between non-Western and pre-colonial cultural materials and postmodernist sensibility has also been gaining acceptance in contemporary cultural studies (Gates). Such efforts as those of Henry Louis Gates to view the signifying monkey narrative mode as a specific African American tropological consciousness and of Houston Baker to identify the blues as a recurrent model for visualizing and narrativizing the human life-world by African American writers are illustrations of non-European discourse that motivate and mime postmodernist sensibility (Baker 1984). Within the framework of folk cultural forms in Africa and Afro-America, evidence abounds, though largely unexplored by critics, to suggest the ever present preoccupation of non-European people from time immemorial with most of the themes of postmodernism. Such verbal gymnastic forms as the African joking relationship, the verbal competition surrounding the Yoruba Ayo game and its African American variant, playing the dozens, the tradition of verbal rivalry in incantation, and the African and African American trickster narrative traditions all enact epistemological and aesthetic traditions that enact the crisis of representation, the problem of dualistic, logocentric imagination, and the importance of heterogeneous and competing discursive practice (Roberts 1989). The appropriation and reuse of some of these discursive traditions, especially of the joking partnership and trickster narrative mode by Langston Hughes in the Jesse B. Semple stories, creates a motivation for viewing this genre of popular fiction and other Harlem Renaissance texts not only as modernist aesthetic response as Baker has ably shown, but also as a mode of miming the themes of postmodernism and its critique of modernism as a partially meta-narrativistic effort (Boyne and Rattansi, 17). The remaining part of this paper will be devoted to the illustration of postmodernist ideas and practice in the Semple stories of Hughes.

The enactment of postmodernist sensibility in the Semple stories is attempted at the level of both content and form. The model selected for the frame event for all the stories indirectly mimes the epistemological strategies often associated with postmodernist cognitive structure and behavior. Hughes's choice of one of many African frames for semiotic play or verbal warfare is appropriate for enacting the notion of meaning or knowledge as contestatory, dialectic, and dialogic. The choice of joking relationship as frame event for the interaction between Semple and the narrator must have been chosen purposely to disclose indirectly the dialectical and dialogical character of ideas. In its original African context, joking relationship or partnership (which is refashioned in the Semple stories) takes many forms. It ranges from two friends engaging in ritual of insults with or without anybody else within earshot to two Ayo players (a Yoruba chess-like game with twelve compartments) engaging before onlookers in a verbal gymnastics of insults and counter insults (similar to playing the dozens). In all cases, joking relationship celebrates the free exchange of ideas that attempt to cancel each other out. In joking partnerships, two individuals that respect each other play out their acceptance of different subjectivities and emotivities. By organizing interpersonal rituals of disagreement, joking partners release pent-up feelings and at the same time mime the plurality of perspectives that characterizes the human life-world.

The relationship between Semple and the narrator is reminiscent of joking partnership. By mutually agreeing to disagree on the nature of racism and ways of fighting or stopping it, the Semple tales depict in a subtle manner the acceptance of the notion of knowledge as a function of semiotic negotiation between different or diverse subjectivities. The debate from story to story between Semple and the narrator enshrines the notion of polyvocality. In addition, Hughes's suturing of tales on the basis of the two principal characters and the fragmentation of action are reminiscent of the trickster-tale cycle. Like the trickster-tale cycle, Hughes's Semple stories enact the fluidity of identity and the eclectic or cumulative and alterable character of cultural knowledge. The way joking partners agree to expand each other's consciousness through juxtaposition of different views held by Semple and the narrator on the same topic illustrates the importance of communication as persuasion or the construction of intersubjectivity. Moreover, the juxtaposition of two discursive styles—the "elitelore" of the narrator and the folklore of Semple—suggests the merger of high and popular discourse as a necessary condition for the creation of social knowledge that will be acceptable across the social spectrum. By fielding in different stories two principal characters that joke about life through verbal exchange, Hughes draws the attention of the reader—highbrow as well as popular—to the need to subject oneself and one's views to debate and criticism by others. By making his two principal characters play language games about life, Hughes provides a popular discourse that thematizes, through the structure of experience, the notion of life and living as semiosis.

While the centrality of dialogue to all the stories shows the importance of plurality of perspectives to knowledge formation, individual tales reveal themes about specific aspects of postmodernist cultural and aesthetic behavior. One of such themes is the notion of the crisis of representation. Contrary to a dualistic, Manichaean, logocentric imagination where reality is marked off in either/or terms, postrepresentationalism or unitivism refers to a non-dualistic mode of cognition and value in which one thing can represent two opposing sides or the point of juxtaposition of opposites (McArthur 1990). As I have argued elsewhere, African cultural discourse is imbued with tropological categories for semiotizing moments of ambivalence and unitiveness. The trickster in both its sacred manner as Esu and its secular context as Tortoise or Ananse or Brer Rabbit represents the possibility of imaging that is nondualistic but negotiatory, nondidactic but dialogic (Sekoni 1994).

Contrary to a dualistic, didactic imagination, the tricksterist imagination provides structures that can straddle oppositions (Wadlington 1975). Unitivism evokes the possibility of a postrational, postrepresentational rhetorical rather than logical truth. Hughes's otherwise simple character is made in several tales to problematize dualism as he argues in several stories for a world view in which opposites are reconciled and simultaneously accepted. For example, in "Less Than a Damn," Hughes through Semple, pushes a unitive imagination on the narrator as he describes his first wife, Isabel, in tricksterist terms:

> At any rate, it were not another woman that caused Isabel and me to break up. It were Isabel. *She was two women in one—one good, one bad.* (*Simple Takes a Wife,* 35)

The notion of twinness of good and evil shows a unitive or incorporative imagination that contrasts with the dualistic, separative sensibility that views the life-world in terms of good or evil. Semple's [that is, Simple's] reference to Isabel as two women in one prefigures a world that needs to be viewed as open and synthetic, and it is reminiscent of the doublesidedness of the trickster figure as a symbol of ambivalence and alterability. Unlike Boyd, the Westernized, rational narrator, and Semple's joking partner, the pre-Western, postrational Semple raises in this passage a major question that problematizes the notion of dualistic and didactic sensibility of elitist discourse.

Furthering the theme of plurality of perspectives, the narrator's quick rejoinder to Semple's "Womens are simple when it comes to a man" with "and men are simple when it comes to women" also critiques a dualistic sensibility. In the same story, Semple's repeated grammatical and spelling problems, "I have *bean*," and his explanation of the use of "I taken by colored people" as a metaphoric renewal of the literal "taken" and as a projection of a marginal experience, all depict the artificiality and social constructedness and context-dependency of language.

In another story, "Two Sides Not Enough," Semple attempts a critique of dualism as he argues with the narrator over the ceiling put on possibilities by binarism in thought and politics:

> Narrator: The right side, or the left side are certainly enough sides for most people to sleep on. I don't know what the trouble is. But, after all, there are two sides to every question.

> Semple: That's just what I'm talking about. Two sides are not enough: I am tired of sleeping on either my left side, or on my right side, so I wish I had two or three more sides to change off on. (*Simple Stakes a Claim*, 61)

The fact that Semple is not being literal about sleeping sides becomes evident later in the story as Semple links the notion of dualism to cultural politics by calling the race problem a function of dualism:

> Once an egg gets in the frying pan, it has only two sides, too. And if you burn the bottom side, it comes out just like the race problem, black and white, black and white. (62–63)

To Semple, racialization is an artificial construction of difference between identity and alterity. The fluidity of identity is replaced by rigidity through the metaphor of frying the egg into distinctive colors through burning. Semple's likening of the human self to a multicolored, incorporative egg and of the social self to the separation of such colors is critical of the dualistic imagination that transforms a unitive experience into a dualistic one. Semple's resistance of dualism and separatism is similar to his objection to his call for a topless and bottomless social space in multiracial America (Bloom 1989).

The notion of the crisis of dualistic and hence didactic representation as a means of divinizing identity and demonizing alterity is further reinforced by Semple's likening of the narrator's meaning determination:

> "I say your semantics makes things too simple" to ideological game playing: "Whatever you are talking about with your *see-antics*, Jack at my age a man gets tired of the same kind of eggs each and every day—just like you get tired of the race problem." (63)

By punning on the word, semantics, Semple uses "see-antics" to critique the creation of social meaning as a ludic activity in which the hegemonist creates and re-creates images of the social process for reasons of the consolidation of its dominance. A similar theme is evident in "Simple on Military Integration." In his discussion of the hypocritical implementation of the constitution by European Americans, Semple reveals, in a satiric vein, the political, manipulative character of cultural discourse in his complaint:

> "I keep telling you, it is time to stop resolving! They have been resolving for two hundred years. I do not see how come they need to resolve anymore. I say, they need to solve. By treating us like humans, that's how." (*The Best of Simple*, 81)

The theme of language as a means of identity formation and promotion at the expense of alterity is also enacted in another story, "Picture for the Dresser." In a story started by Semple's complaints to the narrator about the hegemoniality of signification as the elevation of the self and the repression of the other: "All these plays, dramas, skits, sketches, and soap operas all day long and practically nothing about the Negroes" (*Simple Takes a Wife*, 40). In this story, Semple imagistically shows how identity is promoted in language through a selection of self-marketing clichés. Using photography as a paradigm for self-celebration in discourse—verbal and pictorial—Semple openly laughs at the notion of language as deception with his choice of advertisements in a photographer's studio:

> "If you are not good-looking
> We will make you so"
> "Retouching done," "colored to order—
> expert tinting." (41)

The practice by photographers to "tint" and "retouch" the image of the self for purposes of aesthetization metaphorically thematizes the notion of language, like photography, as self-inscription.

In "Dear Dr. Butts," Semple ridicules the emphasis on the ludic dimension of language by revealing the self-serving, self-promoting, problem-avoiding dimension of the rhetorical display of African American leaders that are in sociocultural terms alienated from their followership. In Semple's analysis of Dr. Butt's rhetoric, cosmetic rather than confrontational language is depicted as capable of only deferring the resolution of the real conflict. In addition to Semple's pun on Butts and "but," he ridicules the diversionary aspect of the self-canceling sentences of the mainstream-loving political leader:

> From the way you write, a man would think my race problem was made out of nothing but buts. But this, but that, and yes, there is Jim Crow in Georgia but—America admits they bomb folks in Florida—but Hitler gassed the Jews. Mississippi is bad—but Russia is worse. Detroit slums are awful—but compared to the slums in India, Detroit's Paradise Valley is Paradise. (*Simple Takes a Wife*, 226)

In this passage, Semple critiques the self-canceling sentences of the middle-of-the-road black leader who joins the language game of politics for the ludic (diversionary) rather than from the transformative (problem-solving) angle. By drawing attention to the diversionary intention of Dr. Butts's verbal jugglery, Semple proposes an alternative in terms of performance and effectivity as he advises Dr. Butts:

> When you answer me, do not write no "so-and-so-and-so but—." I will not take but for an answer. Negroes have been looking at Democracy's but too long. What we want to know is how to get rid of that but. (227)

Other comments on the ludic rather than transformative use of language and other means of signification can be found in his turnin-the-cheek description of the long-winding route of Dr. Butts's ideas to those he purported to be leading:

> I seen last week in the colored papers where you have writ an article for the *New York Times* in which you say America is the greatest country in the world for the Negro race and Democracy the greatest kind of government for all. . . . (224)

In another variant on the theme of ludism in language and politics, Semple illustrates in "Simple's Platform" the role of language as manifesto by depicting the typical politician as a rhetor whose intention is the production of images of temporary persuasion and permanent deception. Simple [Semple] reveals the fact that politics puts more emphasis on verbal gymnastics than problem solving in his reply to the narrator's question:

> Narrator: I know your platform by heart. But what results would you achieve?
>
> Simple: Results? Man, if everything a politicianer puts in his platform resulted in results, there would be no need to hold any more elections. Results has nothing to do with politics. It's the platform. (*Simple Stakes a Claim*, 18)

The crisis of representation, especially the tension between subjectivity and objectivity and the resultant rearrangement of the signifier by the owner of the means of signification, is thematized in "That Powerful Drop." By juxtaposing the scientific (evidential and metonymic) truth of the white-looking individual with the narrativistic truth about the automatic classification of anybody with a trace of black blood as black, Simple enacts the often hidden subjectivity that characterizes cultural knowledge in America's hegemonic social scientific discourse:

> Simple: It's powerful.
>
> Narrator: What?
>
> Simple: That one drop of Negro blood because just *one* drop of black blood makes a man colored. . . . If a man has Irish blood in him, people will say, "He's part Irish! If he has a little Jewish blood, they'll say, He's half Jewish! But if he has just a small bit of colored blood in him, BAM! He's a Negro! Not, He's part Negro." (*Simple Takes a Wife*, 85)

Apart from openly laughing at the arbitrariness inherent in the classification of races in America, Simple is also indirectly raising questions about the privileging of social context over linguistic sign. The role of the emotivity of the owners of the means of signification in the distortion or recoding of both social and scientific signs is revealed for ridicule in Simple's request for a logical explanation by the narrator:

> Simple: Even if you look white, you're black. That drop is really powerful. Explain it to me. You're colleged.
>
> Narrator: It has no basis in science, so there's no logical explanation. (85)

One remarkable aspect of Hughes's Jesse B. Semple stories is the correlation between form and context. While individual stories thematize, as has been described in the preceding discussion, different aspects of postmodernist sensibility, the cycle of tales, like the trickster-tale cycle, reinforces the theme of the plurality of perspectives and the negotiation of social meaning through the periodic reversal of roles between the Narrator and Semple. In some stories, Simple is the leader of thought whose ideas are to be challenged by the narrator. In other stories, the narrator performs the role of the addresser whose ideas are open to scrutiny and critique by Simple as addressee.

The periodic shift between communicator and communicatee, made possible by the frame of African joking partnership, reveals more than any individual story, the postmodernist imagination, especially the fluidity of identity that characterized cultural discourse during the Harlem Renaissance's emphasis on the double consciousness of the writer and his audience. By fielding the narrator as an exemplar of the use of standard English and Semple as a representative of folk, non-Western wisdom, Hughes most economically and very subtly experiments on the possibility of fusing the "twin consciousnesses" of the African American in a multicultural ethos. More importantly, he uses the joking partnership to model the possibility of a dialogue across class lines and to mime such transclass dialogue as a means of evoking an epistemology as well as an aesthetic of negotiation rather than imposition.

WORKS CITED

Baker, Houston A. *Blues, Ideology, and Afro-American Literature: A Vernacular Theory.* Chicago: University of Chicago Press, 1984.

———. *Afro-American Poetics: Revisions of Harlem and the Black Aesthetic.*

Bloom, Harold. *Modern Critical View: Langston Hughes.* New York: Chelsea House, 1989.

Boyne, Roy, and Ali Rattansi. *Postmodernism and Society.* Basingstoke, Hampshire, U.K.: Macmillan, 1990.

Gates, Henry Louis Jr. *The Signifying Monkey: A Theory of Afro-American Literary Criticism.* New York: Oxford University Press, 1988.

Hughes, Langston. *Simple Takes a Wife.* New York: Simon & Schuster, 1953.

———. *Simple Stakes a Claim.* New York: Rinehart, 1953.

McArthur, Tom. *Beyond Logic and Mysticism.* London: Theosophical Publishing House, 1990.

Roberts, John W. *From Trickster to Badman: The Black Folk Hero in Slavery and Freedom.* Philadelphia: University of Pennsylvania Press, 1989.

Sekoni, Ropo. *Folk Poetics: A Sociosemiotic Study of Yoruba Trickster Tales.* Westport, CT: Greenwood Press, 1994.

Wadlington, Warwick. *The Confidence Game in American Literature.* Princeton: Princeton University Press, 1975.

Kindred Spirits and Sympathetic Souls
Langston Hughes and Gwendolyn Bennett in the Harlem Renaissance

Sandra Y. Govan
University of North Carolina—Charlotte

Clearly, as poets and writers, as artists skilled in a variety of forms, Langston Hughes and Gwendolyn Bennett have been accorded different degrees of recognition for their vastly different accomplishments. Each adopted a different method in their respective approaches to art; each had a different understanding of what commitment to art demands from the artist. And as evidenced by their private lives, each had different ideas about commitment to a single individual and about the institution of marriage with its possible effects on the artist. Yet despite these differences between Langston Hughes and Gwendolyn Bennett, both born in 1902 and both the offspring of aspiring and ambitious fathers, there exists a shared sensibility, a sympathetic resonance. This is particularly true when we look at their shared view of the glittering 1920s, the era which perhaps best illustrates that these two highly regarded New Negroes were, in fact, kindred spirits.

If the matrix which shapes the artist can be traced to childhood, it is worth notice that both Bennett and Hughes endured rather unusual circumstances while growing up. The tension between parents and child, the pivotal role of their respective fathers, James Langston and Joshua Robbin Bennett, and the attitude or absence of their respective mothers, Carrie Hughes and

Mayme Bennett, impacted their lives significantly. Hughes announces in *The Big Sea* that he "hated his father" (49), and Arnold
Rampersad makes clear in his penetrating biography that the relationship between father and son was a complex mixture of
love, hate, and guilt (34–59). James Langston, lawyer, was an apparently cold and distant parent, a father who wanted the best
for his son but was incapable of offering guidance or support,
choosing instead to bark orders, issue commands, and denigrate
all the young Langston loved, especially poor and black people.

By contrast, Gwen Bennett seemed to have had the ideal
loving father-daughter relationship with her father, Joshua Robbin Bennett, a teacher and later a lawyer who had moved from
Texas to Nevada to Washington, D.C. Rather than suffering a
distant cold parent, Bennett's problem in her youth, as she once
explained, "was not a case of a child not being loved enough but
loved too much" (interview, March 1979).[1] But Bennett's father
kidnapped her from her biological mother, Mayme Abernathy
Bennett when she was only seven. Young Gwen subsequently
spent the rest of her childhood on the run with her father—a situation which cast Joshua in a dual role—the hero who rescues
his daughter from an unsatisfactory custody judgment; and the
villain, who removes her from and then banishes his daughter's
mother, thus engendering a divided emotional response—
tremendous love and muted hate. Indeed, as is clear from scrib-
bled notes and mementos in her scrap book, young Gwen loved
her father but longed for and missed her mother terribly
(interview, March 1979).

As a consequence of their upbringing, both Hughes and
Bennett led lonely and rather isolated lives as children. Both
spent a significant portion of their early lives away from their
mothers—Langston with his grandmother and Gwen with her
father and assorted "play" relatives. When he rejoined his
mother, Langston found Carrie Hughes an embittered and hard
woman, forced by economic necessity to move frequently in
search of better paying work. Although near poverty was not at
issue, and he certainly never evinced the racial self-hate of James
Hughes, Gwen's father also moved his family about constantly,
staying just ahead of the law while seeking a comfortable niche
for himself. One result of all this movement was that both Ben-

nett and Hughes turned to the arts, to poetry, as partial compensation for their loneliness. Further, despite their personal pain, both were perceived as very likable, very charming, and outgoing youngsters. Also, both had their poetic talents recognized by peers and teachers while high school students; and, both were exceptionally good at masking their true feelings, at internalizing bitterness and refusing to let anger or hostility show. Thus, Hughes could become physically ill when confronted by intense rage—when a doctor diagnoses viral infection and his red blood cell count drops, Langston knows his illness is actually hatred for his father and he takes comfort in the high medical expenses his too frugal father will be forced to pay (Rampersad, 34). In over a dozen interviews with a variety of people, I found few who could ever say they had ever seen Gwen Bennett angry. What has become clear to me from Bennett's sporadic diary,[2] the comments of her friends and co-workers, and the one lengthy interview she granted me before her death is that whenever she felt angry or "stressed," Bennett ate. She masked fear or unpleasantness in healthy eating, in gourmet cooking.[3]

By curious parallel, both Hughes and Bennett attended Central High, predominantly white, and both had their talents recognized in school—academically and with extracurricular activities. Each had a favorite teacher to encourage, and each began developing latent artistic talents in this setting. To be sure, Hughes's Central High was in Cleveland, Ohio, and Bennett's was in Harrisburg, Pennsylvania, but the reverberations of their respective successes resound despite the difference in locale. Hughes wrote poetry for his school's magazine, the *Belfry Owl* (*Big Sea*, 27), read a good deal, and contemplated writing short fiction. In his senior year, he was voted Class Poet and Editor of the school yearbook (52). Actually, Bennett only began her high school training at Central; but her first two years were very successful—she continually made the honor roll. However, when in 1918 she transferred to Brooklyn's Girls High because her father moved the family, her academic progress initially suffered until she adjusted to the new setting. Once adjusted, "Gwennie," like Langston, successfully negotiated within a largely white environment. She was elected to the school literary society and the school drama society—the first Negro to join either—and she won awards for her art work at Girls High; she was also chosen to write the senior class graduation song.

By random chance then, after, in Langston's case, a journey to Mexico or, in Gwen's case, jaunts around the eastern seaboard in tow with her father, both Hughes and Bennett, as high school graduates, managed to converge in New York, at Columbia University, in 1921—the moment when the Harlem Renaissance was beginning to bud. Hughes had mounted a campaign against his father's plan for his future so as to position himself in Harlem—attendance at Columbia had been more or less a ruse. The thought of studying engineering in a foreign language, as envisioned by James Hughes, had been a nightmare for Langston—his dream was Harlem: "I had an overwhelming desire to see Harlem. More than Paris, or the Shakespeare country, or Berlin, or the Alps, I wanted to see Harlem, the greatest Negro city in the world. *Shuffle Along* had just burst into being and I wanted to hear Florence Mills sing" (*Big Sea*, 62–63). Bennett had no campaign to mount merely to see Harlem. Brooklyn's proximity to Harlem is direct via the A Train. However, by choosing to pursue a career in the arts, when her father wanted her to become a lawyer or a teacher—some safe profession—Bennett did have to rely upon some subterfuge and chose Columbia, with its arts education program, as the compromise college. Not surprisingly, given the racial climate in 1921, neither Hughes nor Bennett were particularly happy at Columbia—in fact, they never met there and established few friendships; Langston only stayed one year, while Gwen left shortly thereafter. Hughes, as we know, went to sea; Bennett went to Pratt Institute, back in Brooklyn, to acquire a teaching diploma in applied arts and arts education. But for all its problems, Columbia was close to Harlem, and Harlem was where the action was.

Hughes's descriptions of "the action" Harlem recorded in *The Big Sea*, when, as he put it, the Negro was "in vogue," are well known. He cites the effects of Shuffle Along, the "best of all" theater productions to give a "pre-Charleston kick" to the era; he talks about the rise of celebrated Black entertainers in music, drama, dance: Roland Hayes, Paul Robeson, Florence Mills, Rose McClendon, Bessie and Clara Smith, Louis Armstrong, Gladys Bentley, and Josephine Baker (224). He also mentions the down side—the white invasion of Harlem and the gangster-controlled Jim-Crow Cotton Club. He cites the crass commercial dimension Harlem night spots began to show as the twenties progressed, and he comments upon the idea that New Negro writers also became subverted by the notion that they had to "amuse and entertain white people" and by doing so "distorted and over-colored their material" (226). But Hughes added a caveat to this clear-eyed assessment. "Maybe," he speculates, this happened because there are black "writer-racketeers," those who would exploit themselves or their material for gain. "Maybe . . . but—" he knew almost all of the writers in this period and "most of the good ones have tried to be honest, write honestly, and express their world as they saw it" (227).

From the perspective of distance, years after Hughes penned his memoir, Gwen Bennett spoke of the same phenomena with a similar affirmative clarity. For her, the Harlem Renaissance was a "fun" period, a joyous time where the emphasis was on community, on an exchange of ideas between artists, and where the ways of white folks—authors and party givers—was fodder for gab sessions among black folks. For the young New Negro writers who socialized together this "wasn't a period of drugs or heavy drinking." "Nobody," she declared, "had money for any of those things and most of us were middle-class people anyway with middle-class morals as backgrounds." The chief activity was interaction. "And we just talked incessantly and drank coffee or just ate and talked. We'd go from one place to another and we were always cooking up schemes of what we were going to do and how were were going to conquer the world and who was doing what."[4]

Rather than musicians or representatives of the popular culture, Bennett's touchstones are the artists and race leaders. She recalls cheerfully the one-room apartment Wally Thurman rented where the editorial staff (Thurman, Hughes, Bennett, Nugent, and Aaron Douglass) "cooked up and did most of the work on *Fire.*" Then there were the parties at the "really expensive apartment" of Alta and Aaron Douglass, who "entertained very lavishly all the time." And there were the offices of the "older sponsors of the group" whom the younger artists visited: "We were in and out of the *Crisis* office just like it belonged to us. We

were also in and out of the Urban League office because that's
where Charles S. Johnson was." Actually, Bennett's description
of Johnson coincides with those that paint him as entrepreneur
of the movement:

> Now Charles S. Johnson suddenly came on the scene.
> There he was, the Director of *Opportunity*. I knew nothing
> about him before he was suddenly getting in touch with
> you or calling you for something over the telephone. We
> just didn't go downtown New York without dropping into
> his office. He, already having an accepted job and know-
> ing his way around, how people meet, was always taking
> one or the other of us or several of us out for lunch—long
> two-hour lunches and discussing all kinds of things. So
> that we saw each other all the time—several times a
> week—sometimes as often as every night. (Bennett,
> interview with Govan, 1979)

In large part, the artists' community developing in Harlem
in the early twenties was a very informal network in what Bennett calls a "very informal period [where] everybody knew about
everybody else and what they were doing. We were glad," she
added, "to be alive—it was great to be a part of things . . . and
there were infinite stories."

Mention of Bennett and Hughes with *Fire*, which appeared
in 1926, actually throws off the chronology of my coming-of-age-
in-Harlem scenario just a bit. As indicated earlier, 1921 was a
critical year; 1924 was as well. This was the year both Hughes
and Bennett were "presented," as it were, at the "coming out
party" or "the debut" for Bennett's informal group now dubbed
the "Writer's Guild." The occasion was the Civic Club dinner
sponsored by Charles S. Johnson where "all the younger Negro
writers—[Countee] Cullen, Walter White, [Eric] Walrond, Jessie
Fauset, Gwendolyn Bennett, Alain Locke . . . met and chatted
with the passing generation—Du Bois, James Weldon Johnson,
Georgia Douglas Johnson, etc." (Bontemps, 11). At this same
dinner, C.S. Johnson had also arranged for white editors, publishers, and philanthropists to be present so that connections between black artists and white backers of the arts could be forged.
Now because of his work submitted to *Crisis* since 1921, Hughes

he was presented in absentia, for rather than being there, Hughes was out of the country. Bennett, on the other hand, was very much a part of the festivities; her "occasional poem," "To Usward," was chosen to help launch the new literary movement. Like Hughes, in his poem "Youth" ("We have to-morrow/Bright before us/Like a flame"), Bennett passionately celebrates new directions, a new sense of racial kinship, for the bright and shining New Negro artists.

> Let us be still
> As ginger jars are still
> Upon a Chinese shelf.
> And let us be contained
> By entities of Self . . .
> Not still with lethargy and sloth
> But quiet with the pushing of our growth.
> Not self-contained with smug identity
> But conscious of the strength in entity.
> If any have a song to sing
> That's different from the rest,
> Oh let them sing
> Before the urgency of Youth's behest!
> . . .
> And there are those who feel the pull
> Of seas beneath the skies,
> And some there be who want to croon
> Of Negro lullabies.
> We claim no part with racial dearth;
> We want to sing the songs of birth!
> And so we stand like ginger jars
> Like ginger jars bound round
> With dust and age;
> Like jars of ginger we are sealed
> By nature's heritage.
> But let us break the seal of years
> With pungent thrusts of song,
> For there is joy in long-dried tears
> For whetted passions of a throng![5]

There are several other early twenties poems wherein the

subject matter, the tone or stance of the poet, the themes, and the choice of particular images and motifs illustrate the sympathetic resonance between Hughes's poetry and Bennett's. In his "Song," Hughes admonishes: "Lovely, dark, and lonely one, /Bare your bosom to the sun,/Do not be afraid of light/You who are a child of night" (*New Negro*, 143). Further, the speaker instructs the subject to embrace life by whirling "in the wind of pain and strife." In her "To A Dark Girl," Bennett's speaker also first celebrates, then describes, then admonishes:

> I love you for your brownness
> And the rounded darkness of your breast
> I love you for the breaking sadness in your voice
> And shadows where your wayward eye-lids rest.
> Something of old, forgotten queens
> Lurks in the lithe abandon of your walk
> And something of the shackled slave
> Sobs in the rhythm of your talk.
> Oh, little brown girl, born for sorrow's mate,
> Keep all you have of queenliness,
> Forgetting that you once were slave,
> And let your full lips laugh at fate!

In her poem titled "Song," in lines which, through recurring multiple images of music and dance, echo Hughes' "An Earth Song" or "Dream Variation" ("To fling my arms wide/In some place of the sun,/To whirl and to dance/Till the bright day is done. . . .), Bennett announces:

> I am weaving a song of waters,
> Shaken from firm, brown limbs,
> Or heads thrown back in irreverent mirth.
> My song has the lush sweetness
> Of moist, dark lips
> Where hymns keep company
> With old forgotten banjo songs.
> Abandon tells you
> That I sing the heart of a race,
> While sadness whispers
> That I am the cry of a soul. . . .

After taking us in successive stanzas to the camp-meeting and then to the jazz club, where images of slavery and minstrelsy mix, Bennett's speaker enjoins us all to "Sing a little faster,/Sing a little faster,/Sing!"

Yet poems which reflected an overtly militant or racial attitude were not the only type of poetry these two young poets penned. Both often turned to personal poetry, to nature for subject—using the season, or the night, or the moon to set scene and establish tone. And while the ultimate attitude of their respective speakers may differ, that a resonance exists is unquestionable. Essentially, a melancholy Hughes asks in "After Many Springs" if age has changed him. "Now,/In June,/When the night is a vast softness/Filled with blue stars,/And broken shafts of moonglimmer/Fall upon the earth,/Am I too old to see the fairies dance?/I cannot find them anymore" (*Dream Keeper*, 9). By contrast, in her "Street Lamps in Early Spring," Bennett whimsically describes the night, raising no questions, content with a haunting beauty which again, echoes Hughes. "Night wears a garment/All velvet soft, all violet blue. . . ./And over her face she draws a veil/As shimmering fine as floating dew. . . ./And here and there/In the black of her hair/The subtle hands of Night/Move slowly with their gem-starred light."

Langston Hughes and Gwendolyn Bennett established a friendship that began in the 1920s and remained unimpaired up until Hughes's death in 1967. They read each other's work; they encouraged each other's writing; they lent each other moral support in times of need. Theirs most certainly was a platonic friendship, noncompetitive, nurturing, and mutually supportive. Hughes was by far the better craftsman as poet; he was the artist who recognized he would have to polish his craft if he were to survive as a writer. He also knew he would have to dedicate vast amounts of solitary time to writing. But as a single young man, Hughes had the kind of time and energy to devote to his artistry. As a woman, bound in 1928 by the exigencies of marriage and marital obligations, Bennett was not permitted to remain "foot loose and fancy free." During the early twenties, however, when the New Negro was just coming into vogue, that was another story.

Permit me one last illustration of my basic premise.

Hughes and Bennett both partook of the Paris experience. Hughes, of course, had gone abroad as a seaman and found odd jobs in the black nightclubs then so popular in Paris. In 1925, Bennett went to Paris, on a sorority scholarship and with no additional funds, to study art in the Paris academies. Like Hughes before her, she at first found Paris lovely but Parisians cold; thus, she was lonely as Hughes had warned her could happen, and so she wrote to him, requesting he send copies of his poems once in awhile to allay her loneliness.[6] But when he wrote to her commenting upon his bemused chagrin at the community response to the Carl Van Vechten's introduction and the Miguel Covarrubias's illustrations of his *Weary Blues*, on December 2, 1925, Bennett wrote back, breezily admonishing him not to "mind about the colored liking the Covarrubias cover nor the Van Vechten introduction[;] . . . you're not writing your book only for colored people," she said. "And," she continued, "if they who chance to have a kinship of race with you don't like your things. . . . well, let them go hang." With this advice and these observations, although inelegantly phrased, Bennett anticipates the sentiments Hughes later codified in his famous and often quoted essay which appeared in the *Nation*, "The Negro Artist and the Racial Mountain."

> We younger Negro artists who create now intend to express our individual dark-skinned selves without fear or shame. If white people are pleased we are glad. If they are not, it doesn't matter. We know we are beautiful. And ugly too. The tom-tom cries and the tom-tom laughs. If colored people are pleased we are glad. If not, their displeasure does not matter either. We build our temples for tomorrow, strong as we know how, and we stand on top of the mountain, free within ourselves. (June 23, 1926)

Unquestionably, in the early, heady, and formative years of that flowering of African American arts we now call the Harlem Renaissance, Gwen Bennett and Langston Hughes established an ongoing friendship. This was possible because they respected each other and because they appreciated each other's gifts, each other's accomplishments. They were, after all, kindred spirits and sympathetic souls.

NOTES

1. Gwen Bennett, interview with Sandra Y. Govan, March 1979.

2. Scrapbook, Bennett Papers. Schomburg Center for Research in Black Culture, New York.

3. From diary records, a personal interview, and interviews with several different sources, it became apparent that Bennett used food to allay fear and decrease frustration. Of course, the fact that overeating caused a weight gain brought its own frustrations was a fact Bennett recognized.

4. Bennett, interview with Govan.

5. This poem was first read at the Civic Club dinner; subsequently, it appeared in both *Crisis* and *Opportunity*.

6. Bennett letter to Hughes, December 2, 1925. Langston Hughes Papers. James Weldon Johnson Collection. Beinecke Library, Yale University.

WORKS CITED

Bontemps, Arna. *The Harlem Renaissance Remembered*. New York: Dodd, Mead, 1972.

Hughes, Langston. *The Big Sea: An Autobiography*. New York: Alfred A. Knopf, 1940.

———. "The Negro Artist and the Racial Mountain." *Nation* (June 23, 1926).

———, ed. *New Negro Poets: U.S.A.* Bloomington: Indiana University Press, 1964.

Rampersad, Arnold. *The Life of Langston Hughes: Volume I: I, Too, Sing America*. New York: Oxford University Press, 1986.

Langston Hughes's *Nigger Heaven Blues*[1]

Bruce Kellner
Millersville University

In late October 1926, at the height of its popularity and notoriety, Carl Van Vechten's *Nigger Heaven* ran into some heavy traffic with the powerful ASCAP in an on-coming vehicle that threatened to put the novel permanently out of commission. In innocence or ignorance or both, he had transcribed the words of Papa Charlie Jackson's scabrous song, "Shake That Thing," from a phonograph recording by Ethel Waters, and then he had quoted it in full in one of the occasional speakeasy sequences in his book.

With the threat of a lawsuit pending, Van Vechten avoided disaster by engaging Langston Hughes to compose a twenty-one-line lyric that would fit—line for line—into the printer's plates to replace all three verses of "Shake That Thing." *Nigger Heaven* had already gone through its fifth printing, with 35,000 copies sold and a heavy demand for more, when ASCAP stepped in to protect Papa Charlie Jackson's interests. Timing was crucial, so in desperation Van Vechten had contacted his young friend at Lincoln University.

Langston Hughes was a student then, right in the middle of his fall semester—his second one at Lincoln—but he trained up to New York for a weekend at Van Vechten's apartment and

---

This chapter has appeared in slightly different form in *The Langston Hughes Review* 11, no. 1 (Spring 1992): 21–27.

tailored three verses to fit into the space vacated of necessity by "Shake That Thing." Then, just to avoid the possibility of future reprisals over the fifteen other songs Van Vechten had fool-hardily incorporated into the novel, Hughes wrote substitute lyrics, or snatches of lyrics, for all of them as well, always de-signed to fit directly into the space available and, at the same time, to reflect their tone. It is unlikely that he ever had to mea-sure so carefully his remarkable fluency to someone else's di-mensions, set neither by music nor so much by theme as by some typesetter's ruler. Nevertheless, Hughes's labors resulted in at least a trio of carefully honed lyrics, typical of some of his work during that period, and they did not and do not require Van Vechten's novel to support them. Coming directly after the inci-sive, astonishing poems collected in *Fine Clothes to the Jew*—just the week before his marathon efforts for *Nigger Heaven*, Hughes had given Van Vechten the manuscript—they reflect, however modestly, the direction in which his work had turned in 1926.

Hughes's replacement for "Shake That Thing" and for one or two other lyrics went into a single revised signature for the sixth printing of *Nigger Heaven*—one of those big sheets printed on both sides and folded down to make sixteen pages before it got stitched up with the other signatures. (Of course all that was long ago, before the days of what publishers now call eu-phemistically their "perfect" bindings on their glued-together pages.) The rest of Hughes's work went into the seventh print-ing.

Van Vechten paid Hughes $100, many times that of to-day's equivalent, I suppose, but still a shockingly modest hono-rarium in exchange for keeping his best-selling novel in book-shops across the country. Then he settled with ASCAP out of court for a healthy $2,500, well over one-fourth of the royalties he had accrued. On Friday, November 5, he wrote to Hughes, al-ready back at Lincoln:

> Your poems for Nigger Heaven have gone to the printer. As I assured you before, you are at liberty to use these po-ems in the future in any way you like. You know how grateful I am to you. Everything is settled, and I am *very* tired. Call me when you come to town. Bay crowns to you, Carlo.[2]

Langston Hughes never did use them, nor, so far as I know, were the lyrics ever included in subsequent collections or even documented in his bibliography. Perhaps he only felt he had repaid some debts and favors and let it go at that. He had owed the novelist several. Van Vechten had introduced Hughes to a wide, white public by arranging for a selection of his poems to run in *Vanity Fair*, the most popular, trend-setting magazine of the twenties. He had persuaded his own editors, Blanche and Alfred A. Knopf, to publish Hughes's first collection of verse, *The Weary Blues*, and he had supplied a persuasive introduction to the book. He had underwritten some of the expenses for *Fire!!*, that one-issue magazine, radical then, legendary now, which Hughes, Wallace Thurman, Zora Neale Hurston, and other black intellectuals had produced. On occasion he had supplied young artists and writers with casual handouts too. Moreover, Hughes admired *Nigger Heaven*, privately as well as publicly, in conversation and in print, although he told Alain Locke he thought it read as if it had been written by "an N.A.A.C.P. official" because it was so "pro-Negro."[3] Still, he chose not to preserve his *Nigger Heaven* lyrics beyond the confines of Van Vechten's novel. Perhaps, because of the violent reaction against it, he decided in hindsight that subsequent silence was preferable.

In any assessment of Hughes's early work, however, the lyrics ought to be acknowledged and examined as successful examples of his early manner, to say nothing of his ingenuity. Admittedly, they are minor exercises in the major mode of parts of *The Weary Blues* and *Fine Clothes to the Jew*, like Czerny and Hanon limbering up the fingers for more accomplished performances.

"Shake That Thing" becomes "Born an' bred in Harlem,/ Harlem to duh bone./Ah say, born an' bred in Harlem,/ Harlem to duh bone./Early every mornin'/You can hear me moan . . ." (248). It is a superb illustration of Hughes's own succinct definition of the blues: "sadness . . . not softened with tears but hardened with laughter."

He had clearly indicated his attitude about the blues in a letter to Van Vechten well over a year earlier, and indeed he had indicated indirectly how they played in his own work:

> The Blues. . . . always impressed me as being very sad,
> sadder even than the spirituals because their sadness is
> not softened with tears but hardened with laughter, the
> absurd, incongruous laughter of a sadness without even a
> god to appeal to. In the Gulf Coast Blues one can feel the
> cold northern snows, the memory of the melancholy mists
> of the Louisiana low-lands, the shack that is home, the
> worthless lovers with hands full of gimme, mouths full of
> much oblige, the eternal unsatisfied longings. (see n. 3)

There was a "monotonous melancholy," he continued, "an ani-
mal sadness" in all Afro-American jazz, "almost too terrible at
times," and he remembered hearing a native band in the
Kameroon in Africa when two boys circled a dance floor, their
feet stamping endlessly an incessant rhythm while their bodies
turned and swayed, "like puppets on strings," he said. The horns
"moaned in monotonous weariness—like the weariness of the
world . . . ," but the drums provided a "deep-voiced laughter for
the dancing feet." It all reminded him of a verse sung by one of
the boys with whom he had shipped out for Africa:

> I went to the gipsy's to get mah fortune tol',
> I went to the gipsy's to get mah fortune tol',
> Gipsy done tol' me, "Goddam your un-hard-lucky soul."[4]

It is a good example of that "sadness . . . not softened with tears
but hardened with laughter," predicated on the rich interplay of
literal and figurative metaphor, not only "worrying the line" but
"worrying the word," as Nora Holt used to call it.[5]

Here, similarly, are Langston Hughes's long-forgotten
lyrics for Carl Van Vechten's *Nigger Heaven*, beginning with
"Born an' bred in Harlem, Harlem to duh bone." The rest of it is
a woman's lament, rueful but proud, for an absent lover, buried
in the middle of which is a fine, ironic turn on color and its ram-
ifications in two spectrums:

> Ah'm a hard-boiled mama
> From Lenox Avenue.
> 'Taint nobody's business
> What Ah do.
> Sometimes Ah feels lonesome,
> Sometimes Ah feels sad,
> But Ah can't keep no lover

Cause Ah'm evil and bad.
Ah found me a pap,
A high yaller too.
He lef' me in duh mornin'
With his face all black and blue.
Ah drinks bad liquor
An' Ah likes et strong.
Ah'm a hard-boiled mama,
So doan do me no wrong. (248–249)

It was not the kind of material likely to have endeared Langston Hughes to Countee Cullen, who had wondered, in his *Opportunity* review of *The Weary Blues* earlier that year, "whether the jazz and blues pieces were really poems at all"; nor, a year later when *Fine Clothes to the Jew* was published, as Arnold Rampersad has pointed out, to William M. Kelley, who thought such material "reeked of the gutter and the sewer"; nor to Joel A. Rogers, who called it "piffling trash."[6] To many black readers in the twenties, the blues idiom—in art at least—was inappropriate, subversive. If the "Talented Tenth" of the race, in which W.E.B. Du Bois and his generation put such stock, dared to kick up a heel or shuffle along rather than march, in putting its best foot forward, the danger that white America might hear the wrong rhythm could be only magnified. Elsewhere in that sixth printing of *Nigger Heaven*, Hughes rewrote a popular ditty guaranteed to invite dismay:

Ah can shake et up,
Ah can shake er down,
Ah can put et on duh flo'
An' turn et roun'. (249)

To replace the familiar "Ef you hadn't gone away," in which a woman tears up her man's photograph and mumbles about doing nothing while he runs around town, Hughes supplied a poem that seems to me more lacerating than any blues or popular lyric Van Vechten might have lifted from a phonograph record for his novel. It could be set to music even now; but it will stand alone—as not all song lyrics can—without the benefit of the music, because of the parallel accretions in a prosody that urge the deliberate banalities Hughes puts in the mouth of his persona to cut any reader's quick. One might with impunity

identify it as an Afro-American sonnet deriving from earlier
variations on the form, whether Hughes knew it or not. I am not
referring to the number of its lines: there are eighteen, not fourteen; nor its rhythmic pattern: syncopations borne of both spirituals and blues replace iambic pentameter; but its rhyme scheme
reinforces its architecture, first self-containing the proposition or
problem in the first ten lines, then using a new rhyme as transition from the tenth to the eleventh, introducing the similarly self-
contained solution or response in a trio of asseverations. Its closure, repeating the opening lines, only turns the sonnet into a
song:

> Baby, lovin' baby,
> Won't you come home today?
> Ah been cryin' an' a-cryin'
> Ever since you went away.
> Duh good Lord knows
> You took mah heart,
> You took et lak a toy
> An' you broke et all apart.
> You kicked me roun' an' slapped mah face,
> But nobody else can take yo' place.
> Ah'm gonna send a telegram
> In a yaller envelope,
> Gonna take a drink o' gin
> To keep up hope.
> Gonna git a sofa piller
> An' kneel down an' pray,
> Oh, Baby, baby baby,
> Won't you come home today? (277–278)

Here the tension that a conventional blues structure achieves, in
repeating an opening line before its variation, is played on verbally by repeating a rhythmic structure but varying the image.
The delay in a poetic rather than a musical closure builds its
tension in that grim descent from public telegram to private so-
lace, first in booze and then, as a euphemism for sex, in prayer. I
do not mean to suggest that Langston Hughes had the time or
took the time to ponder over a richer subtext in both form and
content than is immediately apparent, but, instead, that he was
already sufficiently accomplished to dash off an inconsequential

lyric masquerading as an inarticulate lament that is in truth a poem.

All of his remaining lyrics were incorporated into *Nigger Heaven's* seventh printing, "Harlem to duh bone" and whatever else fell in the signature that contained it having been rushed into the sixth. In between the two runs, there was time to set his work in the other printer's plates as well. The ubiquitous "Yes, Sir, That's My Baby" became Hughes's "Oh, How I'm Aching for Love," and "I Had Someone Else before I Had You" became his "What Does It Matter That I Want You," in which love "is like a sweet lump of sugar in a cup of hot tea: it doesn't last very long" (35). The well-known "Nobody knows duh way Ah feels dis mornin'" he replaced with "Ah wants to hop a train an' go where duh town is clean" because "Folks roun' heah is so low-down mean" (52). Many of these were only two-liners, squibs here and there in the novel, but Hughes often seems to have given them as much attention as he gave to full-length lyrics; brevity never curtails art. He replaced "Not on the first night, baby/An' mebbe not a-tall" with "Takes a better man than you/to make a sweet mama shout!" (137). But whether he wrote a full-length lyric or merely a filler, his words reinforced Van Vechten's text. Sometimes Hughes only revised the form and kept the content, always with economy and often with *double entendre* guaranteeing a smile. "Singin' Sam from way down South/Sounds lak he got a organ in his mouth" is a marked improvement on both counts over "His voice sounds lak time. I mean duh organ time,/An' when he speaks his music ease mah troublin' min'" (144). "I'll take her back if she wants to come back" wasn't much of a lyric to begin with, so *Nigger Heaven* was none the worse when Hughes added this throwaway:

> She did me dirty,
> She did me wrong,
> She kept me fooled all along.
> But I've been so lonesome
> Since she went away
> That if she'll come home
> I'll let her stay. (207)

Van Vechten had used a wonderfully raunchy song he had learned from Nora Holt, a reigning Harlem glamour queen, later

a respected music critic, "While you're sneakin' out, somebody
else is easin' in," but it was no loss to his novel when Hughes replaced it with this one:

> You ain't gonna ride no chariot tonight
> 'Less you take your sweet mama along!
> I say, Ben Hur, you ain't goin' out
> Till you listen to this song.
> I know you been drivin'
> To some other girl's door
> But I'm gonna see to it
> You don't drive there no more.
> You ain't gonna ride no chariot tonight
> 'Less you take your sweet mama along. (246–247)

Van Vechten took the precaution, too, of cutting out "Nobody can bake a sweet jelly roll so fine, lak mine" because
another acquaintance, blues singer Clara Smith, had had a big
success with it just then. Hughes's replacement preserves the
implicit smut but extends the metaphor rather than merely
padding the couplet:

> Ah'll tell duh world Ah can stir it roun',
>   Stir it roun',
> Takes a gal lak me to bake a cake up brown.
>   Cake up brown. (281)

All of these songs or snatches of them had been interpolated in the novel to serve as ironic commentaries on incidents in
the plot, or to serve to advance the action. Uncannily, despite the
brief period during which he composed his pieces, Hughes usually managed an even closer affiliation with Van Vechten's intentions; often enough, the verses are so organically right for the
text that it is difficult to think of the novel without them. At least
once, however, Langston Hughes was too successful; or perhaps
I mean that at least once, however, he failed. When the heroine is
obliged to sing an earnest love song, at one point in the novel,
Van Vechten had employed James Weldon Johnson's "Sence You
Went Away," a now-forgotten popular ballad. When the girl
finishes singing, her beau says, "That's a good tune, but a bad
sentiment," and he's certainly right. In response to Hughes's
substitute lyric, the beau's assessment is wrong, however, be-

cause the poet ennobled his own deliberately "bad sentiment" in a deliberately wrenched syntax and deliberately clumsy grammar to give it a touching dignity:

> Roses used to was
> So sweet, so sweet, dear.
> Sunshine used to was
> So bright, so bright.
> Now there ain't
> No roses nowhere, dear—
> Seems lak duh sun
> Done stopped a-givin' light
> Cause you had to go away. . . . (142)

Nigger Heaven's initial popularity—a hundred thousand copies in the first three years—resulted not only in subsequent reprints but in several translations. Some were made immediately, based on the first printings, but others resulted in Langston Hughes's appearing in foreign tongues as early as 1929. Oddly, however, the Danish translator was assisted by Hughes's friend, Richard Bruce Nugent, but employed all those songs protected by ASCAP. ("Shake That Thing" in Danish, incidentally, is "Vil du Riste."[7]) But Hughes did appear in Italian: "Born an' bred in Harlem,/Harlem to duh bone" became "Nata e crescuita ad Harlem/Harlem fino alle ossa," and "a hard-boiled mama" is "una mama provata all'avventura"[8]: "a tasty mama ready for anything." I wonder what German and Polish and Czechoslovakian made of those phrases, for those translations also employed Hughes's lyrics.

In all subsequent American and English editions of the novel, a note has been included to indicate that "the songs and snatches of Blues sung by characters"—with a list of the page numbers for them—"were written especially for *Nigger Heaven* by Mr. Langston Hughes," either on the copyright page or at the end as part of Alfred A. Knopf's colophon. Since the lyrics are buried in a novel dismissed by Van Vechten's detractors and only mildly endorsed by his few enthusiasts, they have been overlooked—but undeservedly, I think. Written at a time "when Harlem was in vogue,"[9] as Langston Hughes himself later described those "splendid drunken twenties,"[10] they are "Harlem to duh bone," emblematic of a time and place, and worth preserving as modest footnotes to a long and distinguished career.

NOTES

1. Page references in parentheses following Langston Hughes's verses, and to passages from the songs they replaced, refer to the first, sixth and seventh printings, as indicated, of Carl Van Vechten's *Nigger Heaven* (New York: Alfred A. Knopf, 1926).

2. Carl Van Vechten, *"Keep A-Inchin' Along": Selected Writings About Black Arts and Letters,* ed. Bruce Kellner (Westport, CT: Greenwood Press, 1979), 255.

3. Quoted in Arnold Rampersad, *The Life of Langston Hughes, Volume I: 1902–1941: I, Too, Sing America,* 2 vols. (New York: Oxford University Press, 1986), I: 134.

4. Quoted in Van Vechten, 46–47.

5. Bruce Kellner, "Sterling A. Brown: *Building the Black Aesthetic Tradition [rev.], American Literature* 58. 2 (May 1986): 293.

6. Quoted in Rampersad, 140.

7. Carl Van Vechten, Niggerhimlen, trans. Kelvin Lindemann (Inderhafter, Denmark: Aschehour Dansk Forlag, 1933), 205.

8. Carl Van Vechten, *Il Paradiso dei Negri,* trans. Gian Dauli. (Milan, Italy: Modernissima, 1930), 290.

9. Langston Hughes, "When Harlem Was in Vogue." *Town and Country* (July 1940): 64.

10. Carl Van Vechten, *Fragments from an unwritten autobiography* (New Haven: Yale University Library, 1955), 3.

Commencement at Lincoln University, June 1943, left to right: Manuel Rivero, Langston Hughes, J. Newton Hill; seated far right: Carl Sandburg

Playgram, "Shakespeare in Harlem," Forty-first Street Theatre, New York, NY, February 1960

The "Race, Culture, Gender" panel, Dickey Hall, Lincoln University, left to right: Dr. C. James Trotman, Professor Cheryl Wall, Professor Joyce Joyce

A student views the conference displays in the Langston Hughes Memorial Library exhibit cases

Ms. Doris Mayes, mezzo soprano, presents a musical demonstration in Dickey Hall, Lincoln University, accompanied by Dr. Alvin Amos. Left to right: the "Hughes's Poetry and Music" panel: Dr. Ezra Engling, Dr. Steven Tracy, Mr. Raoul Abdul

Jackson State University, 1952. Standing (left to right) : Arna Bontemps, Melvin Tolson, Jacob Reddix, Owen Dodson, Robert Hayden. Seated left to right: Sterling Brown, Zora Neale Hurston, Margaret Walker, Langston Hughes

THE WORLD OF LANGSTON HUGHES MUSIC
Concert of Poems, and Musical Settings
Sponsor, All Seasons Art

The Langston Hughes Community Library & Cultural Center
February 12, 1984   Sunday 4:00

102-09 Northern Boulevard, Corona NY 11368, 212 / 651-1176

Queensborough Public Library

"The World of Langston Hughes Music," The Langston Hughes Community Library & Culture Center, Corona, NY, February 12, 1984

Commencement at Lincoln University, June 1943; recipients of honorary degrees, left to right: Langston Hughes 1929, Nathan F. Mossell 1879, Herbert E. Miller 1910

*Race, Culture, and Gender
in Langston Hughes*

Race, Culture, and Gender in Langston Hughes's *The Ways of White Folks*

Joyce Ann Joyce
Chicago State University

Set in Iowa, New York, New Jersey, the Florida coast, New England, Ohio, Chicago, and Georgia, Langston Hughes's *The Ways of White Folks* emerges as a collection of satirical short stories that gives a comprehensive glimpse of the various manifestations of race relations throughout the United States and within all the different class strata of white society. Cited in Volume I of Arnold Rampersad's *The Life of Langston Hughes*, some of the reviews of the collection demonstrate the highly mixed reactions of white readers to any black literature that acutely depicts white hypocrisy, corruption, or insensitivity. While Herschel Brickell in the *North American Review* commented that the collection represented "some of the best stories that have appeared in this country in years" (290), and Horace Gregory asserted that the stories revealed a "spiritual prose style and an accurate understanding of human character" (290), Sherwood Anderson, on the other hand, wrote, in the *Nation*, "My hat is off to you in relation to your own race" (290). Anderson, according to Rampersad, thought that the whites in Hughes's collection were caricatures. "And Martha Gruening, a prominent white liberal, deplored the fact that [Hughes] saw whites as either sordid and cruel, or silly and sentimental'" (290).

Both the negative and highly positive reviews testify to the breadth and depth of Hughes's collection. The fourteen stories that make up *The Ways of White Folks* explore the psychological depth of the multileveled behavioral codes that govern the interaction between blacks and whites and that describe the inferiority/superiority paradigm that makes up white consciousness. The reaction of white readers and critics attests to the degree to which the title of the collection draws attention away from Hughes's black characters, whose purpose is to illuminate "the ways of white folk." Because the artistry of Hughes's stories differs greatly from Richard Wright's—particularly in tone and mood—we do not quickly see the similarity between Hughes's and Wright's depiction of racism. Although *The Ways of White Folks* is satirically humorous and progresses through the beautiful merger of prose and poetry, it, too, like much of Wright's naturalistic fiction, reveals a world in which whites do not understand their behavior, in which they are not in touch with themselves, and, thus, in which they are both physically dangerous to blacks and psychologically dangerous to themselves and to blacks.

While Wright's *Uncle Tom's Children*, published five years after Hughes's collection, features two black women protagonists only (Sarah in "Long Black Song" and Aunt Sue in "Bright and Morning Star"), Hughes's *The Ways of White Folks* presents numerous black and white women characters, demonstrating the integral role white women play in propagating social and moral racial codes that affect the lives of both black women and men. In fact, a black or a white woman is either the protagonist or a pivotal character in every story in *The Ways of White Folks*.

In describing the multifaceted manifestations of racism found among all classes of whites across the United States, *The Ways of White Folks* emerges as an ingenious analysis of the interrelationship between race, class, and gender. *Racism*, interestingly enough, is a cultural and political phenomenon rooted in the merger of the concepts of race and culture. Whereas *race* denotes a "local geographic or global human population distinguished as a more or less distinct group by genetically transmitted physical characteristics" or a "group of people united or classified together on the basis of common history, nationality, or geographical distribution" (*American Heritage Dictionary*, 1020), *culture* refers to "the totality of socially transmitted behavior patterns, arts, beliefs, institutions, and all other products of human work and thought characteristic of a community or population" (*American Heritage Dictionary*, 348). *Racism*, then, signifies the merger of race and culture. In *The Ways of White Folks*, Langston Hughes adroitly demonstrates how white people with a common history and shared physical characteristics stifle their own lives and those of the blacks around them by continuing the legacy of behavioral patterns and beliefs that propagate their self-hatred, their hypocrisy, and their insensitivity and the paradox of inferiority/superiority that describes their interaction with blacks.

What is perhaps most striking about *The Ways of White Folks* is both the amount of space Hughes gives to women characters and his depiction of how racism and class have affected their lives. Despite Hughes's lack of any mention of his sexual life in *The Big Sea* and in *I Wonder as I Wander,* despite the confusing critical discussions about his alleged homosexuality, and despite his condescending, perhaps even sexist comment "Girls are funny creatures" in reference to Zora Neale Hurston in *The Big Sea*, his characterizations of both black and white women in *The Ways of White Folks* reveal a profound mind artistically capable of identifying with the intricacies of female consciousness and of censuring female participation in the cultural behavioral patterns that stifle their humanity. Even though all of the fourteen stories in the collection contain female characters, both black and white, and though eleven of the stories feature black women characters, it is interesting that three of the most powerful and moving stories in the collection have black women as major characters. It is through the experiences of these black women that we can clearly view "the ways of white folk."

Of the fourteen stories, "Father and Son," "Cora Unashamed," and "The Blues I'm Playing" emerge as those with the most sustained treatment of black female characters. "Cora Unashamed" and "Father and Son," appropriately begin and end the collection. Despite the fact that Hughes titles the collection *The Ways of White Folks*, he begins and ends the book with black women characters who are strikingly different from each other and who serve as points of reference for the female charac-

ters in the other stories. Except for Oceola in "The Blues I'm Playing," all the other black women characters lack the dignity and
wisdom of Cora in "Cora Unashamed" and struggle to overcome
Cora's poverty as well as Coralee Lewis's entrapment in "Father
and Son."

While Cora of "Cora Unashamed," the protagonist of the
first story, is self-assured, courageous, loving, and wise, Coralee
Lewis, the mother figure in "Father and Son," is disappointingly
weak, and her failure to censure her white lover/master before
his death results in his death as well as the death of her two sons.
Though Cora represents a traditional depiction of the black
woman, Coralee emerges as a rather strikingly nontraditional,
equally as convincing portrait of the black woman before and
after slavery. During slavery, Coralee is just a young girl on the
then young Colonel Norwood's plantation. He marries a young
woman from whom he becomes isolated, and the slaves begin to
gossip because Norwood and his young wife fail to have children. Norwood, like John Dutton in Margaret Walker's *Jubilee*,
goes to the slave quarters to have his sexual desires fulfilled by
Livonia, who also has four black lovers because she loves to love.
Coralee's reaction to talk of Livonia"s affair with Norwood
clearly suggests that some black women during slavery welcomed a sexual union with their masters: "Cora heard all this
and in her mind a certain envy sprang up. Livonia! Huh! Cora
began to look more carefully into the cracked mirror in her
mother's cabin. She combed her hair and oiled it better than before. She was seventeen then" (208). When Cora took milk to the
Big House after this, "she tried to look her best" (208). Later during a party at the Big House, Coralee takes a walk out in the
woods near the house. Young Norwood, who is restless, takes a
walk and ends up near Coralee, sitting under a huge oak tree.
Norwood approaches her, asks who she is, takes her face in his
hands, and has sex with her.

It is not appropriate to say that he seduces her. For Coralee
clearly desired Norwood long before he knew of her existence.
When Coralee is pregnant with her first child, she tells her
mother of her situation. Her mother's response suggests the
black woman's dilemma before and after slavery. Coralee's
mother says, "It's better'n slavin' in the cotton fields. . . . I's

known colored women what's wore silk dresses and lived like queens on plantations right here in Georgy. . ." (210). Although Coralee's actions and her mother's attitude are not characteristic of all African American women during and after slavery, they do suggest the attitude and behavior of some black women, those women who fell prey to the conditions of their environment.

Hughes, however, goes further than to demonstrate that all slave women were not repulsed by the sexual advances of their masters. He also shows the price they and their offspring paid for this sexual union. After Bert, one of Coralee and the Colonel's four children, shoots the Colonel, he then shoots himself in order not to be lynched by the mob that pursues him. As a result of all the trauma, Coralee retreats inside herself and goes mad. The lynch mob not only lynches Bert, but his brother Willie, too. Willie had always acted humbly in order not to antagonize whites. Set during early Reconstruction, "Father and Son" dramatizes the complexity of the black woman's history. For as a young slave woman, Coralee has no dreams of a life outside the plantation. A sexual liaison with the slave master opens up opportunities that allow for a specious level of comfort. Thus, after slavery Coralee is able to convince Norwood to send her four children away to school, yet she and those of her children who returned to the plantation never moved beyond the status of slaves in Colonel Norwood's perception and treatment of them. Coralee completely acquiesces to his racism and attempts to instill her fears and cowardice into her offspring.

Even though Colonel Norwood and his son Bert are the two main characters as suggested by the title of the short story, Coralee's situation helps us appreciate the depth of the Colonel's racism and the inexorable cultural taboos that prevent him from marrying her and accepting her offspring as his own.

Quite unlike Coralee, Cora, the central character of "Cora Unashamed," challenges white society in very different ways. Despite the fact that Cora's financial situation and her home environment are as wretched as Coralee's, on some level Cora realizes that she can make choices about how she lives her life. Cora's brothers have deserted the family leaving Cora to take care of an ailing mother and an alcoholic father.

Hughes dramatizes Cora's self-assurance and her courage by contrasting her with the wealthy Studevant women for whom she works as a domestic in a small, rural town in Iowa, 150 miles from Sioux City. While the Studevant women are hypocritical, elitist, and insensitive, Cora is humble, strong, and generous, particularly with her sincere love for people. Cora and Mrs. Studevant give birth, around the same time, to daughters, both of whom Cora nurses. After Cora's baby dies, she devotes all of her attention and love to Jessie, the Studevant child, who is seriously neglected by her mother and the rest of her family. When Jessie becomes pregnant, she seeks comfort in Cora, who tells Mrs. Studevant of her daughter's pregnancy. Mrs. Studevant first faints and later collects herself enough to tell the town that she and Jessie are going on a shopping trip to Kansas City, where they actually go for an abortion.

Jessie returns from the trip a different person. And her death is due more to a broken heart over the loss of her child than from any surgical complications. Hughes uses natural imagery to suggest Jessie's and Cora's wholesomeness as opposed to the narrowmindedness and unnaturalness of Mrs. Studevant, her mother, and her older daughter. When we first meet Cora, the narrator explains that she was "like a tree—once rooted, she stood, in spite of storms and strife, wind, and rocks in the earth" (3–4). And when there is a discussion about Jessie's going away to normal school after high school, the tree again represents Cora's stability, strength, and her natural ability to love: "Cora hated to think about her going away. In her heart she had adopted Jessie. In that big and careless household it was always Cora who stood like a calm and sheltering tree for Jessie to run to in her troubles" (9). Natural imagery also suggests the difference between Jessie's and Cora's wholesome attitude toward love-making and pregnancy and the Studevants' attitude. The narrator describes Cora's thoughts as she thinks of Jessie: "Then Spring came in full bloom, and the fields and orchards at the edge of Melton stretched green and beautiful to the far horizon. Cora remembered her own Spring, twenty years ago, and a great sympathy and pain welled up in her heart for Jessie, who was the same age that Josephine would have been, had she lived" (13).

A moving portrayal of the interrelationship between race, culture, and gender, "Cora Unashamed" dramatizes how the Studevant women's elitism and insensitivity cause them to ignore Jessie's needs and motivate their attempt to instill their cultural values in Jessie. And just as it is forbidden for a young, unmarried woman of their class and race to become pregnant outside of wedlock, it is equally forbidden for the Studevants, like Colonel Norwood, to consider Cora, a black woman, a human being even though she nurses their child and is responsible for the full care of their home.

The Studevants are not as wealthy as the Mrs. Dora Ellsworth of "The Blues I'm Playing." When Mrs. Ellsworth discovers Oceola Jones, a young black woman violinist, she is enthralled with Oceola's blackness as much as she is with Oceola's musical skill. Mrs. Ellsworth appoints herself as Oceola's patron and attempts to control Oceola's life. When she learns that Oceola does not charge rent to her lover/boarder, Mrs. Ellsworth assumes that Pete Williams, a Pullman porter, saving money for medical school, is exploiting Oceola. Having always had the many comforts that money can buy, Mrs. Ellsworth denies herself an emotional life and is thus incapable of understanding or appreciating Oceola's relationship with Pete. Mrs. Ellsworth is a voyeur who lives vicariously through the lives of those she patronizes, though she needs to control them in order to do so. Because she is racist and elitist, she attempts to lure Oceola away from Pete by taking her to Paris and convincing her to move away from Harlem, where she frequently plays for churches and at parties.

Mrs. Ellsworth, however, is unsuccessful in destroying or even penetrating the core of Oceola's love for herself, for Pete, for black people, and for black culture. Oceola informs Mrs. Ellsworth that she and Pete are going to get married and invites Mrs. Ellsworth to the wedding. But Mrs. Ellsworth informs them that, although she will be unable to attend, she will send a nice gift. It seems that she must go to Florence to meet her new young protégé, "a charming white-haired boy from Omaha whose soul has been crushed in the West" (117). But Mrs. Ellsworth believes herself to be superior to Oceola and the latest protégé. Rather than seeing them as human beings, she unknowingly treats them as objects to comfort her in her loneliness. Yet, Oceola, like Cora in "Cora Unashamed," is not ashamed of her emotional life or her culture. She uses her music to celebrate life rather than to avoid it.

In "The Blues I'm Playing," Langston Hughes displays his deep knowledge of music and the arts in both the African American and Euro-American traditions. But his love of black music, well illustrated at the end of "The Blues I'm Playin," suggests that Hughes is not just writing short stories so that white people can read about themselves; he also writes to pay tribute to the lives of the many "ladies' maids and truck drivers, laundry workers and shoe shine boys, seamstresses and porters" (*Big Sea*, 233) that he met at rent parties in Harlem and on Seventh Street in Washington, D.C. Oceola's playing a blues song at the end of the novel and Mrs. Ellsworth's preference to stand and look at the stars rather than sing of love nicely contrasts Hughes's idea of art with the Euro-centric notion of "art for art's sake." His portraits of black women like Cora, Coralee, and Oceola underscore the reason why Hughes is one of the few black writers read continuously by a large number of blacks in the underclass. They recognize that he is writing to them as much as about them. And the attention he gives to black women in *The Ways of White Folks* reveals Hughes's understanding that the African American woman is the chord that unites the historical triad of race, culture, and gender.

WORKS CITED

"Culture." The American Heritage Dictionary of the English Language. Boston: Houghton Mifflin, 1971.

Hughes, Langston. *The Big Sea*. 1940. Rpt. New York: Hill & Wang, 1963.

———. *The Ways of White Folks*. 1934. Rpt. New York: Vintage Books, 1971.

"Race." The American Heritage Dictionary of the English Language. Boston: Houghton Mifflin, 1971.

Rampersad, Arnold. *The Life of Langston Hughes: Volume I: 1902–1941: I, Too, Sing America.* New York: Oxford University Press, 1986.

"For All the Kids to Come":
The Troubled Island of William Grant Still and Langston Hughes

C. James Trotman

West Chester University

Artistic collaborations have been one of the more successful means for critics and the general public to peer beyond the formal structures and myths of artistic creativity. Bontemps and Cullen in St. Louis Woman, Rodgers and Hammerstein's *The King and I*, and, of course, Hughes and Hurston's *Mule Bone* are familiar examples.

With the association of Langston Hughes and William Grant Still, we are fortunate to have some existing correspondence that privileges us again to gain some insight into the way ideas and influences of various sorts are at work in the poetry of Hughes, the musicianship of Still, and the collaboration they achieved in presenting in 1949 the first opera in a major production in which libretto and score were created collaboratively by Afro-Americans. The title for this talk comes, in fact, from a letter the peripatetic Hughes sent to Still, dated June 8, 1937, from Salt Lake City. Hughes tells Still about his itinerary and brings him up to date on their opera, *Troubled Island*. He concludes the letter with a characteristic note on the culture's role for shaping the future. "It was swell seeing you and Verna again [Verna being Still's second wife], and I am sure we are going to have a beautiful and effective opera that all the world will love, and that will do a great deal to advance Negro culture and music and self-respect for all the kids to come."

Not much has to be said about the dependence of music on lyric poetry or on the particularities of black music on Hughes's work. It is, however, necessary to remind ourselves about the interpretive modes used to discuss this influence. John Lovell reminds us of the epic character of black music in his celebrated work *Black Song: The Forge and the Flame.* Amiri Baraka deepens the epistemological context for it in *Blues People,* and, of course, the precision Ralph Ellison brings to it through his theoretical discussion about the blues as both symbol and cultural signifier in "Richard Wright's Blues," with its echoes of Eliot's "Tradition and the Individual Talent" (Ellison, *Shadow and Act,* 22).

The collaborative relationship between Hughes and Still is first dated in 1934 while Still was in Los Angeles beginning the first of several Guggenheim and Rosenwald fellowships that freed the composer to concentrate on his music. Still had been working on one socially oriented dramatic piece called *Blue Steel* when he received a welcomed interruption by Hughes, who had finally sent him the libretto he had finished. It was based on the life of the Haitian Jean Jacques Dessalines and was eventually to be called *Troubled Island.*

Both Hughes and Still had experienced similar disappointments with other artists. Still had been turned down by other contemporary poets in his request for operatic libretti. Even the then famous Countee Cullen was unresponsive to Still's requests, despite the efforts of Alain Locke to intercede on Cullen's behalf. Hughes, similarly, had experienced frustrations with composers, particularly New Jersey's Clarence Cameron White, who turned to other poets.

Yet it would be misleading to suggest that out of the background of common disappointments their relationship was smooth and without its own sources of tension. Part of the tension derived from their genuine and unconcealed philosophical differences. According to Judy Still, William's daughter and the discriminating custodian of many of his papers, her father was a conservative to moderate on racial issues. As she has written, "He believed that prejudice was only an affliction of the ignorant and the inept, and that the majority of the white people would abjure hatred when led to enlightenment by the intelligent Afro-Americans. It was his conviction that, if the colored man excelled in all areas of endeavor and made significant contributions to science and to culture, and if he made strides without terrorism or social protest, the result would be the best of all possible worlds where all races lived together in peace. He tried, artistically, to express emotions and common feelings, rather than to depict racial bitterness" (J. Still, January 13, 1992). However conservative Still's racial politics may appear now, he certainly was not without social and racial sensitivity.

William Grant Still was born on May 11, 1895, on the country plantation named Piney Woods, which was partly owned by the elder William Grant Still in Woodville, Mississippi. While his father died surprisingly and mysteriously the year young Still was born, the younger, nevertheless, received a middle-class upbringing by his mother, Carrie Fambro, who left Mississippi shortly thereafter to live and raise her son in Little Rock, Arkansas. From all accounts, raising a family at first without a father did not keep Carrie from following the old adage of "sparing the rod and spoiling the child." She not only was the disciplinarian in the house, she was also proudful enough, so the story goes, that she upbraided a rail conductor whom she knew for calling her by her first name in a public setting (Arvey, 15).

So Still, like Hughes, would find some of his most ardent support coming from the women in his life. Carrie saw to it that his talents were put to use—not for music initially but in medicine. Still enrolled in Wilberforce in September 1911, only to discover and rediscover that his real interest lay in music, he shortly thereafter wrote his mother and told her of his decision to enroll in Oberlin (Arvey, 37).

By September 1915, Still was married for the first time to Grace Bundy, and by 1922, although with four children, his marriage was failing. Nevertheless, Still was developing his skills as a musician and composer and attracting the attention of R. Nathaniel Dett, who was teaching at what is now Hampton University, and the legendary W.C. Handy, with whom Still spent the summer of 1916 playing with Handy's Memphis band. In addition to these figures, one must add to the list of influences in the shaping of the collaboration the name of Philadelphia's first African American Rhodes Scholar, the aesthetician Alain Leroy Locke.

As he did in the lives of so many others, Locke was both a gauge and adviser to Grant Still. He saw in Still another talent for his well-known views on art and the Afrocentric potential for bringing about a "new order"; in other words, specifically the kind of representative thought that was presented in the *Survey Graphic* issue of 1925, one year before Carter G. Woodson would inaugurate and make it possible for us to institutionalize Black History celebrations by the day, the week, the month—maybe even more in the future. Locke's new order was revisionist and catalytic. It was an attempt to rearrange the historical myths which undergirded American thought in order to make room for this new icon, the New Negro. The setting was urban America; the place was symbolized through and in Harlem; and the people were the new artists and theorists who were the first to introduce modernism into the vernacular of the movement which we now call the Negro or the Harlem Renaissance.

Several of the letters I have seen show that even with Still, Locke persisted in his efforts to prosyletize for the "New Negro." (I don't think I need to remind this audience of the deconstruction of the phrase under Locke's very determined effort to rewrite the image of the African American in the style of the day. But if a refresher helps, let me refer you to Joel Williamson's *The Crucible of Race*.) In 1937, Locke wrote Still to congratulate him on the debut of a symphony by Still he had just heard in Philadelphia. After congratulating him, Locke stated that the formal symphonic development should remain the virtue; however, he added, "[I]f we are to represent the Negro and for that matter mid-modern life, there must be fresh and unexpected improvisational movement not the predictable steps and return re-tracings of the traditional style" (A. Locke to W.G. Still, December 20, 1937). This is a point worth noting in view of the negative critical response to the opera, which contributed to its brief stage life.

From Chicago in 1940, Locke wrote pointedly about the collaborative effort between Hughes and Still that "it is a most significant thing—quite symbolic really—both in the nature of the collaboration and the spiritual significance of the universal appeal, above race, to common denominator democracy" (A. Locke to

W.G. Still, August 31, 1940). There were also solicitations: to compose the music for a number of themes, lynching being one of them; the other was to join Locke at Howard University in the Music Department, which did not happen (A. Locke to W.G. Still, July 8, 1941).

The libretto for the opera comes originally from *Drums of Haiti*, a play that Hughes had written in the twenties. By the time Hughes and Still had reached the point of collaboration, *Troubled Island*, as it was now called, had much of its earlier developments. The libretto taken from the play is about the first president of liberated Haiti and, of course, the island people themselves; nevertheless, it is a study in frustration. But from the perspective of the libretto, we find a common occurrence when Hughes sets his mind on a specific place. To a large extent, the place is informed by history. Haiti, like Kansas, Missouri, New York, or Moscow has spacial as well as symbolic significance in Hughes's consciousness.

One of a number of reference points is Haiti's connection to the history of re-colonization that helped shape the earliest debates over nationalism and assimilationism in this country, from as far back as Thomas Jefferson's plan in the 1790s to the even earlier suggestions from the membership of Philadelphia's free, black community in the 1780s. In broad terms the question of African emigration is a question in two related parts, one of power and the other of identity.

In the first quarter of the eighteenth century, Jean Pierre Boyer, then president of Haiti, extended an invitation to free blacks in the country to emigrate to Haiti with assurances that "the descendants of Africa would find a brotherly reception in Hayti, should they choose to come there." It was not an unattractive offer because some black leaders thought about the possibility of uplifting their status, which they thought was impossible in the colonies given the increase in the number of slaves arriving with each cargo ship. Some in fact went, but the experiment did not last very long. Black people found it hard to adjust to the socio-political climate; furthermore, President Boyer withdrew his assistance because he began to fear that the immigrants might overthrow his regime. There is nothing in the copy of the libretto that I have seen to suggest that Hughes was working his way through this particularly diasporic and political dimension of the African in the Americas, but he surely knew of the historic significance of Haiti because he had been there in the thirties (Rampersad, I, 204). Part of Hughes's canniness as a writer, moreover, was to take his readers and listeners before points of historical significance and then permit them to explore the point of when and where they entered black culture's defining moments. The entry point becomes its own way for another kind of collaboration.

The subject of the play is the life of Haiti's first emperor, Jean Jacque Dessalines. The setting is Haiti in the Napoleonic era of 1791, and the libretto covers four separate acts. The hero is characterized by a number of qualities that one would associate easily with Hughes and others of his generation who were defining the racial self by unraveling some of the historiography that had stripped the human image of the black person in the world. Dessalines was in real life an illiterate slave born on a plantation. He joined the slave revolt of 1791, the point at which the story begins. He fought under Toussaint, and when Toussaint was captured and sent to France, Dessalines led a successful rebellion against the French. It is important to note, I think as Hughes would have, that the liberation of Haiti made it the second independent nation in the Western hemisphere behind the United States. Dessalines became president on January 1, 1804, but soon proclaimed himself emperor. Two years later he was murdered.

The notes to the score that I have seen bear some interesting racial and cultural points. The cast is described as follows: "The entire cast, with the exception of Duval, Stenio, and Claire, the Mulattoes, are pure Haitians of direct African descent, and therefore quite dark." And these are some of the lines spoken by Martel, a flat but important character because of his links to Africa, addressing Dessalines:

> Remembering Africa, The Black Man's land where Tall and proud black kings and chiefs hold sway. Well do I remember Africa. Well do I remember too that most unlucky day the slavers came and stole me away. Dark hold of a slave ship over the Western ocean we came in chains to this island where men are slaves. Chains where men are slaves. And now like dew upon this troubled island fall our tears. Men are slaves. All is darkened with a pall for we are slaves and Africa is far away. So long so far away! Here we know

only slavery! Chains! Beatings! Pains! Slaves of the world are we, children of misery! Gain. Never! Keep them afar. Let Haiti be a land where black men are free—a world for you and me in my old age, Jean Jacque, an even bigger world than that I dream. A world where all men will live well. Listen my son! I dream a world where man no other man will scorn, where love will bless the earth and peace its path adorn. I dream a world where all will know sweet freedom's way, where greed no longer saps the soul, nor avarice blights the day. A world I dream where black or white, whatever race you be, will share the bounties of the earth, and every man is free where wretchedness will hang its head and joy, like a pearl, attends the needs of all mankind. Of such I dream—my world! My world!

When *Troubled Island* was finally performed on March 31, 1949, by the New York City Opera Company, it was a dream come true for the librettist and the composer, both of whom had invested much time and talent in the project, with the hope that they were to open new doors and remove traditional barriers for blacks in the arts. Locke was right about the significance of the opera, but he may have undervalued the role race and culture appeared to others in the opera's brief life.

On opening night *Troubled Island* received a standing ovation from the audience with, according to reports, numerous curtain calls from the audience. *Time Magazine* called it a "triumph"; the *Boston Post* placed it in the ranks of the best of American operas; the National Association for American Composers and Conductors gave Still a citation for outstanding service to American music. The response of the New York critics, however, guaranteed that the opera would not succeed. Mostly, they did not like the music or the dancing. Olin Downes's review in the *New York Times* of April 1, 1949, is generally representative. He wrote that "there were some Negro voices in the chorus of this opera by a Negro composer and Negro librettist, which enhanced the quality of the choral tone." He went on to say that "very little is new." He did, however, enjoy the dancing. Other critics described it as lacking in an idiom distinctive to the composer, calling it "turgid" and "lacking in originality." But Downes was like other New York critics in saying little if anything about the libretto. The opera closed after only three performances and with it the collaborative effort of Still and Hughes. Why did *Troubled Island* fail? Clearly there were some extenuating circumstances

Making use of some theories on marginality and contextuality that are available to us today, and adding to the menu some homegrown troubled islands of our own in the familiar social and psychic archipelagoes of anti-blackness and racism, it is worth examining the opera in its historical setting.

The year was 1949. In April of that year, Robeson had given his now famous remarks in Paris at the World Peace Conference on colonial peoples and the denial of their rights. The press took his words and turned them into the "I love Russia" theme that systematically muzzled and silenced Robeson. It also was the year that the House Un-American Activities Committee wanted to hear testimony from prominent blacks—some would see it in ritualistic terms of paying homage to the gods—leading eventually to the repressions of the McCarthy Era. In this social and political climate, Hughes and Still faced more than the usual artistic tension. One cannot overlook the racial and cultural component that Locke identified. It was first of all the story of black revolution in which a black man's troubled existence is surrounded by images of the past in which Africa, its pride, its past glories, and memories are part of the opera's inner drive.

The play is decidedly Afrocentric—as we might say these days—because of the interior compass of the play. The black male leadership in the play is "tall, powerful, and black." In the light of the public villification that Paul Robeson was experiencing, this surely must have had some psychological impact. The joy of Africa in the opera is everywhere; indeed, when the word "Africa" drops out of the libretto, so too does the moral focus. The moral touchstone, the Euripedes equivalent of the blind seer Tieresias, is Martel "of ancient wisdom, born in Africa." The gods are black; the religion of Voodun is based on West African religious practices; and the minor gods are African, as is the geography evoking them with references to Senegal and the Congo. Moreover, the people are black, and with typical Hughesian ambiguity over color, the mulattoes are not only figures of mistrust, they are figures without any loyalty at all except to their own.

The point is that the opera is very black, very "Negro," if we remain historically faithful to the racial signifier of the time. It debuted at a time when the black communities' most cherished public figures, like Robeson, were under public scrutiny and real political attacks. Moreover, Still's wife, Verna Arvey, has some interesting observations about this response to the play and to the political climate. Of course, one would expect her to be an advocate, and she was, but like her husband, she believed that a considerable amount of political pressure existed against any opera by Negroes succeeding artistically—and, specifically, against Hughes—in sufficient quantities to ensure the failure of *Troubled Island.*

Arvey, *In One Lifetime,* her 1984 biography of Still, refers to several conversations, some taking place even before the opera was performed, in which she was told that *Troubled Island* was marked for failure. Helen Tigpen, a black woman singer who discussed the review with a New York critic, was told, "Well, we are only going to let just so many Negroes through." In language that is understandably tentative, Arvey then points out that the government had ordered the United States Information Agency to stop making copies of *TI* and to pull back the copies that had been distributed. Ms. Arvey does not go further except to cite Still's disappointment and to say that he returned to composing (Arvey, 143).

Whether Arvey is right about a conspiracy is hard to say, given the slim evidence that she presents. But she does point to an ideological beachhead that was surfacing, in which a repressive political climate was resonating within the body politic at the moment *Troubled Island* was being launched. Moreover, while the government had recorded and distributed *Troubled Island,* it unexplainably pulled back all of its copies when the New York producer started making inquiries into the prospects of the New York company traveling abroad.

The story of Hughes and Still does not end here, although collaboration ceased. Each went on to carry out an exemplary artistic life. Ten days after the first performance, Carl Van Vechten wrote Still in what may be seen as a fitting epitaph to these artists and to their collaboration—and maybe even a fitting testimonial to the character of cultural determination to keep hope alive. Van Vechten wrote Still in obvious response to the critics of *Troubled Is-*

land: "Never be discouraged. Endurance and patience are more necessary assets to the artist than talent. I have read so many shifty reviews of operas after the first night. Only Rodgers and Hammerstein are exempt. *Troubled Island* will probably drift into success, but better start work on another opera at once. . . . Some day there will be a Negro repertory company when it will be a simple matter to get such works on the stage. . . ."

WORKS CITED

Arvey, Verna. *In One Lifetime.* Fayetteville: University of Arkansas Press, 1984.

Ellison, Ralph. *Shadow and Act.* New York: Random House, 1964.

Rampersad, Arnold. *The Life of Langston Hughes.* 2 vols. New York: Oxford University Press, 1986, 1988.

Williamson, Joel. *The Crucible of Race: Black/White Relations in the American South Since Emancipation.* New York: Oxford University Press, 1984.

Achieving Universality through Simple Truths

Donna Akiba Sullivan Harper
Spelman College

If we take Langston Hughes at his word as expressed in *I Wonder as I Wander*, he sought "to write seriously and as well as [he] knew how about the Negro people, and make that kind of writing earn for [him] a living" (5). To some, this goal seemed both inadvisable and detrimental. Writing exclusively about African Americans appeared foolhardy because that focus ignored the more popular assimilationist goals of the earlier decades in this century. Moreover, such exclusivity was sure to lead to literary failure. After all, the most successful writers achieved universality—wrote for the ages, spoke across national boundaries. Any black writer who would become canonized must surely transcend his own race! In one of his final news columns and two years from the end of his life, Hughes argued against such an attitude.

> When I am, as author, speaking at writers conferences, or giving advice to young writers, particularly Negroes, some of them sometimes say, "Why be Negro writers? Why not write just about people? Why limit ourselves?" In their seeking to achieve a sort of integrated univer sality, I say that a fictional character can be ever so ethnic, ever so local and regional, and still be universal in terms of humanity. And I give Simple as an example. He is a Harlemite whose bailiwick is Lenox Avenue, whose lan-

guage is Harlemese, and whose thoughts are those of Harlem. Yet in print Simple is known on the Boulevard Saint Michel in Paris, in Soho in London, on the Unter den Linden in Berlin, and I expect on the Ginza in Tokyo since some of his stories are in Japanese. Folks in far off lands identify with him.

When readers identify with Simple, I imagine they identify with him first as a man, another human being, rather than as a *colored* man. ("Simple Again")

Hughes defends his own achievement of universality by citing his friend Jesse B. Semple. The continued publication of *The Best of Simple* affirms that its popularity exceeds the years of its creation. The international translations of Simple stories and productions of *Simply Heavenly*, the stage version of Simple, indicate continued global interest in this figure from Harlem.

In the broader scope of Hughes's work in many genres, the attendance of scholars, students, creative artists, educators, and lay people at conferences devoted to examining and celebrating Langston Hughes, testifies that Hughes's goal to write about black people was both wise and successful. Langston Hughes study conferences—held at University of Missouri in Joplin in 1981, at City College in New York City annually, and at Lincoln University in Pennsylvania in 1992—have attracted participants from all over the United States and from some parts of the world. The Langston Hughes Society was founded in 1981 and lists hundreds of members. The *Langston Hughes Review* remains in publication ten years after its founding. These many bits of evidence reveal that writing seriously about African American people proved successful for Hughes.

Moreover, Hughes's success has taught subsequent generations of writers valuable lessons about universality. While we once associated broad human values which were not limited to one place or to one period of time only to such classics as Shakespeare's *Romeo and Juliet* or Jane Austen's *Pride and Prejudice*, we can now trace both critical and popular appraisals of the Simple tales and find the same praise being offered to Langston Hughes's portrayal of this Everyman from Harlem.

By reviewing the kinds of authorial, aesthetic, and critical decisions which led to Hughes's creation of Simple, contemporary readers can see how similar declarations and choices have arisen from other critics and African American writers. Furthermore, readers can note the scholarly and popular evidence that Simple has indeed remained vibrant and believable beyond both his era and his geographical and political boundaries.

First of all, while Langston Hughes had already become firmly established as a writer by 1943 when he introduced the Simple episodes as occasional features in his weekly column in the *Chicago Defender*, that venue provided Hughes's first regular access to an almost entirely African American audience, not of the priviledged and elite but of average people. Thus, while Hughes had needed to consider the broader American reading public with his short stories for the *Saturday Evening Post* or for his earlier collections of short stories such as *The Ways of White Folks*, by 1942 when he began his "Here to Yonder" column in the *Defender*, he could address a black audience every week. He could use the language—even the slang—of the black readers of the Negro press. He could focus upon the issues which his African American audience wanted to discuss, and he could include humorous references which this specialized audience would appreciate. Thus, we must acknowledge that Hughes launched his Simple character as a voice which would address a black audience. He did not envision the global community as his audience, nor did he think of his columns as surviving to speak through the ages.

Secondly, this Jesse B. Semple who grew to fill five separate volumes and who remains in print today in *The Best of Simple*, now in its umpteenth printing, did not emerge after a summer of sequestered planning, drafting, and revision, as did Sandy in *Not Without Laughter*. By contrast, Simple began as a 500-word experiment for a new weekly column. He began without a name, and he came before the public with no better introduction than being Hughes's "Simple Minded Friend." His reappearance in the column remained experimental for many months, and only after the public affirmed his veracity and his importance did Hughes pursue the steps necessary to transform this occasional visitor into a regular and leading character.

This transformation in some ways resembles the appearance of character Steve Urkel in "Family Matters," a weekly situ-

ation TV comedy currently on ABC. This Urkel originated as a
one-episode feature, but the public and the critics rapidly promoted him to a necessary regular cast member. Moreover, actor
Jaleel White is now branching off into other features, including
his own one-hour special. Steve Urkel may not have achieved
universality, but his transformation from a one-episode character
to a major "star" resembles Jesse B. Semple's transition from experimental and occasional feature in "Here to Yonder" to the
protagonist of five books and a musical!

While Hughes did *not* set out in his February 1943 debut of
his "Simple Minded Friend" to craft an enduring fictional character, in *Crisis* of June 1941, he *had* already proclaimed "The
Need for Heroes." In this essay Hughes declared that some author needed to celebrate the "compelling flame of spirit and
passion that makes a man say, 'I, too, am a hero'" (184). "The
Need for Heroes" plainly stated Hughes's belief that some writer
needed to offer literature which would present African American
heroes. He wanted literature which would provide

> great patterns to guide us, great lives to inspire us, strong
> men and women to lift us up and give us confidence in the
> powers we, too, possess. . . . Negro heroes and Negro
> heroines—who may or may not always speak perfect En-
> glish but who are courageous, straightforward, strong; . . .
> whose words and thoughts gather up what is in our own
> hearts and say it clearly and plainly for all to hear. (185)

Hughes envisioned literature which would speak to contemporary readers, inspiring them, but would also linger to inform future generations that African Americans had been great men and
women. Indeed, appearing fresh in the wake of Richard Wright's
Native Son, Hughes's essay "The Need for Heroes" and his creation, Simple, argue convincingly that Bigger Thomas failed to
represent all of black America. Hughes wanted to show heroism
and greatness, yet he saw such greatness among the common
people.

> We need in our books those who have known the day-af-
> ter-day heroism of work and struggle and the facing of
> drudgery and insult that some son or daughter might get
> through school and acquire the knowledge that leads to a

> better life where opportunities are brighter and work is
> less drab, less humiliating, and less hard. (206)

Filled with his own belief in this need for heroes, in November 1942, Hughes launched his weekly column in the *Chicago Defender*. The Simple Minded Friend who meandered onto the pages of the black press offered his opinions and narrated episodes about his life because that is what such a fellow might do. Yet, because Simple confronted life and "did not die a suicide, or a mob-victim, or a subject for execution, or a defeated humble beaten-down human being" ("Need for Heroes," 184), he stimulated gratitude and empathy from the masses of black readers who recognized in him either themselves or someone else that they knew. Blyden Jackson thoroughly praises Simple's ordinariness:

> Whether or not he is truly like most ordinary Negroes,
> he is certainly, in both form and substance, what many or-
> dinary Negroes were at least once prepared to concede
> without rancor that they thought they were. At least, to
> that extent, Simple must be accounted a folk Negro's con-
> cept of the folk Negro. (72)

This folk Negro aimed at a mass black audience and discussed the strange contradictions of American democracy for a Negro living in the World War II era.

In 1950 William Gardner Smith offered his opinions on "The Negro Writer: Pitfalls and Compensations." He urged black writers to render their tales authentically, thereby reaching all people:

> The Negro writer, if he does not make the tragic error of
> trying to imitate his white counterparts, has in his posses-
> sion the priceless "gift" of thematic intuition. Provided he
> permits his writing to swell truthfully from his deepest
> emotional reaches, he will treat problems of real signifi-
> cance, which can strike a cord in the heart of basic human-
> ity. He will be able to convey suffering without romanti-
> cizing; he will be able to describe happiness which is not
> merely on the surface; he will be able to search out and
> concretize the hopes and ambitions which are the basic
> stuff of human existence. And he will, in Hemingway's
> words, be able to do this "without cheating." For the basic

fact about humanity in our age is that it suffers; and only
he who suffers with it can truthfully convey its aches and
pains, and thwarted desires. (76)

This same William Gardner Smith, who was a reporter for the
Pittsburgh Courier, praised the publication of *Simple Speaks His
Mind*: "Because most of these columns were written for a Negro
audience, they are uninhibited, intimate, to the point." Evidently,
he felt that Hughes had indeed "truthfully conveyed" the "hopes
and ambitions which are the basic stuff of human existence."

Twenty years after launching the Simple episodes, ten
years after publishing the first book-length collection of Simple
tales, secure in his own reputation, Langston Hughes sat face-to-
face with James Baldwin and several other writers, both black
and white. They came together in 1961 to broadcast over WABI-
FM their opinions of "The Negro in American Culture." This
gathering came only two years after Baldwin's offensive review
of Langston Hughes's *Selected Poems*, in which the younger
writer decried that "the American Negro" found "the war between his social and artistic responsibilities all but irreconcil-
able." With Baldwin's bitter words still remembered, Hughes
expounded upon his own views of universality. He began by
reading a passage from a recent episode of Simple. Then Hughes
discussed his views as a writer:

> I very often try to use social material in a humorous form
> and most of my writing from the very beginning has been
> aimed largely at a Negro reading public, because when I
> began to write I had no thought of achieving a wide-
> public. My early work was always published in *The Crisis*
> of the NAACP, and then in *The Opportunity* of the Urban
> League, and then the Negro papers like the *Washington
> Sentinel* and the *Baltimore [Afro] American*, and so on. And I
> contend that since these things, which are Negro, largely
> for Negro readers, have in subsequent years achieved
> world-wide publication—my work has come out in South
> America, Japan, and all over Europe—that a regional
> Negro character like Simple, a character intended for the
> people who belong to his own race, if written about
> warmly enough, humanly enough, can achieve uni-
> versality.

> And I don't see, as Jimmy Baldwin sometimes seems to
> imply, any limitations, in artistic terms, in being a Negro. I
> see none whatsoever. It seems to me that any Negro can
> write about anything he chooses, even the most narrow
> problems: if he can write about it forcefully and honestly
> and truly, it is very possible that that bit of writing will be
> read and understood, in Iceland or Uruguay. (90–91)

As Arnold Rampersad notes in volume two of his biography of
Hughes, the major difference between Baldwin and Hughes was
that unlike Baldwin, Hughes had "deep confidence in blacks and
a love of them (two qualities that could not be divorced)" and
these qualities "would allow a black writer to reach the objectivity toward art that Hughes saw as indispensable" (297).

Clearly, Hughes intended to write "forcefully and honestly
and truly" through his creation of an average African American
who refused to veil his sentiments. As the title of the first volume
of collected stories proclaimed, *Simple Speaks His Mind*. Yet, his
honesty and his intense concentration upon his own Harlem
lifestyle has proved universal. Other writers and critics support
this approach to global and timeless appeal.

Toni Morrison shares Hughes's view of universality. In a
1977 interview with Jane Bakerman, Morrison states that she in-
tends in her writing to talk about or write about "those Black
people the way I knew those people to be" (59). She specifically
avoids explaining things, insisting that clear, specific writing
transcends the need for explanation:

> If I could understand Emily Dickinson—you know, she
> wasn't writing for a *Black* audience or a *white* audience; she
> was writing whatever she wrote! I think if you hone in on
> what you write, it will *be* universal . . . not the other way
> around! (59)

Clearly, Morrison eschewed becoming what her character Guitar
Bains would refer to as "'universal,' human, no 'race consciousness'" (*Song of Solomon*, 224). Both Morrison and Hughes clearly
proclaim and then demonstrate that intensely race-conscious literature can communicate universal truths to any active reader.

In "Black Orpheus," originally the preface for an anthology edited by Léopold Sédar Senghor in 1948, Jean-Paul Sartre
describes *Negritude* as "black men . . . addressing themselves to

black men about black men." He then goes on to stress what he
sees as the universal significance of Negritude, insisting that the
white man "can gain access to this world of jet," because black
writing is "actually a hymn by everyone for everyone" (16).
Having followed virtually the same formula, writing the Simple
episodes in newspapers addressed to black people and talking
about black people, Hughes read and highlighted Sartre's discussion. As translated by John MacCombie, "Black Orpheus"
appears in the Autumn-Winter 1964–1965 issue of the *Mas-*
sachusetts Review. This issue was included in Hughes's personal
collection and was bequeathed to the special collections of the
Langston Hughes Library at Lincoln University. On the binding
of Hughes's copy of the journal, in his traditional green ink,
Hughes had noted "Black Orpheus." Thus, Hughes had read and
wanted easy notation of Sartre's observations.

C.W.E. Bigsby notices that African American works, like
Jewish works, had begun to represent the universal person.
Aware of the potential danger in such a pronouncement, Bigsby
explains:

> This does not mean that the black writer is producing as-
> similationist works "which are universally human" be-
> cause they are about white characters and white prob-
> lems—a prospect which the cultural nationalists view with
> some alarm. The potency of the Negro's metaphorical role
> derives precisely from its ethnic specificity. (26)

Such ethnic specificity certainly did not strike "universal" chords
at Simon and Schuster when the editors decided to publish *Sim-*
ple Speaks His Mind. The initial readers celebrated the racial authenticity which provided the white reader "a prickling sense of
being an eavesdropper" on a black conversation. Indeed, they
plainly enjoyed "a key-hole type of fascination for a white man,
and it opens a door freshly, revealingly, invitingly, unostenta-
tiously" (Readers). By offering to the mainstream American reading public these Simple tales, Hughes allowed an ordinary "folk"
Negro to speak plainly about the issues which concerned ordinary black folk. What impressed the white readers for Simon and
Schuster in the late 1940s was the authentic Negro voice which
addressed the concerns of those years. What has survived for
forty years, however, is an authentic everyperson's voice which

echoes through the ages. The injustices and the humorous meth-
ods of meeting such injustices speak for oppressed people in any
place. And who among us does not feel oppressed sometimes?

For evidence that Simple achieved universality, readers
should note the multiple translations of the Simple stories and
acknowledge the favorable critical responses. The entire Fall
1985 issue of the *Langston Hughes Review* treats the subject of
Langston Hughes in translation. Included in this issue are Harry
L. Jones's discussion of Simple in Danish and Soi-Daniel W.
Brown's discussion of Simple in German. Later issues of the
Langston Hughes Review provide Michel Fabre's comments on
Simple in French and a news service report about the amputees
in Kartoum, Sudan, who appreciate the Simple stories.

The Danish translations of Simple emphasize common
bonds. Harry Jones reports that in his translation of Simple,
Michael Tegn notices similarities between himself and the
Harlemite:

> Tegn recognizes that Simple is already as much a Dane as
> he is a black American, for Simple is the universal little
> man who has intelligence enough to see the disparity be-
> tween a society's preachments and practices, and who is
> articulate enough to express his personal dilemma and
> frustrations at the difference. (24)

Jones goes on to credit Hughes with the necessary beginning:
"Had not Hughes himself created a universal outsider, an Ev-
eryman, if you will, Tegn would not have been able to render
Simple as such" (25).

Similarly, Soi-Daniel Brown assesses Hans Rogge's article,
"Die Figur des Simples im Werke von Langston Hughes." Brown
finds that Rogge "recognizes the reason for the popularity and
success of Hughes's Simple stories: Hughes' mastery of dialogue
and ability to make demands on the American public and government in an apparently naive and innocuous manner" (35).

Michel Fabre summarizes the French response to Simple.
"To gauge the scope of [Hughes's] literary reputation in Paris,
one need only go through the varied, but unanimously laudatory
remarks of French critics—of every ideological affiliation—when
L'Ingenue de Harlem, a collection of selected Simple stories, was
published the Spring of 1967" (26). Fabre also highlighted com-

ments from Dahomean and Ethiopian commentators who attested to the authenticity of Simple.

Current generations of readers continue to laugh with Simple at the woes of his landlady, the boldness of his Cousin Minnie, and the ironies of governmental inconsistencies. These new generations of readers empathize with Simple, too, when he recalls the tough love of his Aunt Lucy when she gave him his final whipping, or when he reflects on the sadness of dying alone. The global enjoyment and the half-century of enjoyment suggest that this ordinary Negro from Harlem, this Simple Minded Friend, has spoken his plain truth to the ages. We celebrate the weekly column which satisfied and delighted readers of the Negro press in the 1940s, 50s, and 60s, but we also rejoice that Hughes launched a character who became a folk hero. We applaud Langston Hughes for achieving universality through Simple truths.

WORKS CITED

Bakerman, Jane. "The Seams Can't Show: An Interview with Toni Morrison." *Black American Literature Forum* 12 (Summer 1978): 56–60.

Baldwin, James. Review of *Selected Poems. New York Times Book Review.* March 29, 1959.

Bigsby, C.W.E., ed. *The Black American Writer: Volume I: Fiction.* Baltimore: Penguin, 1969.

Brown, Soi-Daniel W. "'Black Orpheus': Langston Hughes' Reception in German Translation (An Overview)." *Langston Hughes Review* 4.2 (Fall 1985): 30–38.

Campbell, Joseph. With Bill Moyers. *The Power of Myth.* New York: Doubleday, 1988.

Fabre, Michel. "Hughes's Literary Reputation in France." *Langston Hughes Review* 6.1 (Spring 1987): 20–27.

Hughes, Langston. *I Wonder as I Wander: An Autobiographical Journey.* New York: Hill & Wang, 1956.

———. "The Need for Heroes." *Crisis* (June 1941): 184–185+.

------. "The Negro in American Culture." [A Transcript.] Bigsby, ed. 79–108.

------. "Simple Again" [or "Simple's Birth"]. *New York Post*. October 29, 1965.

"International." [News item in "Notes & Reports."] *Langston Hughes Review* 6.1 (Spring 1987): 60.

Jackson, Blyden. "A Word About Simple." *CLA Journal* 11 (June 1968). Rpt. in Jackson, *The Waiting Years: Essays on American Negro Literature*. Baton Rouge: Louisiana State University Press, 1976.

Jones, Harry L. "Simple Speaks Danish." *Langston Hughes Review* 4.2 (Fall 1985): 24–26.

Morrison, Toni. *Song of Solomon*. New York: Signet, 1977.

Rampersad, Arnold. *The Life of Langston Hughes: Vol. II: 1941–1967: I Dream a World*. New York: Oxford University Press, 1988.

Readers #3 and #7. First Report. "Simple Speaks His Mind: Readers' Reports." Hughes Manuscripts, Mss 3537. James Weldon Johnson Collection. Beinecke Rare Book & Manuscript Library, Yale University.

Sartre, Jean-Paul. "Black Orpheus." Translated by John MacCombie. *Massachusetts Review* 6.1 (Autumn/Winter 1964–1965): 13–52.

Smith, William Gardner. "The Negro Writer: Pitfalls and Compensations." *Phylon* 1950. Rpt. in Bigsby, ed. 71–78.

------. Review of Simple Speaks His Mind. *New Republic* 123 (September 4, 1950): 20.

The Physics of Change in "Father and Son"[1]

R. Baxter Miller

University of Georgia

> What happens to a dream deferred?
> Does it dry up
> like a raisin in the sun?
> Or fester like a sore—
> And then run?
> Does it stink like rotten meat?
> . . .
> Maybe it just sags
> like a heavy load.
> *Or does it explode?*[2]

Langston Hughes, probably the most brilliant poet of African American dreams, voices curiosity about the physical world. Riddled with decay and stench, the world contains an almost magical mystique of purpose. At times the qualities seem to defy even the certain principles of gravity. For physics has seemed to be the science of energy and of the relation of it to matter, though the definition is imperfect. To understand energy would mean to have a command of all physics as well. The science of energy, in the most complete sense, includes all science. Natural philosophy, the earlier name for physics, once included a greater range of other sciences. But eventually they became specialized as chemistry, metallurgy, astronomy, meteorology, and geology. Since about 1870 physics has become narrowed to the current scope, though the process of disciplinary separation continues. Certain areas of physics, for example, developed during the construction of the nuclear bomb during World War II. Soon afterward they began to divide off into an independent branch of nuclear engineering designed to produce nuclear power. Nevertheless, the interconnections between physics and other sciences are so intimate that it is impossible ever to separate them completely. And, in tracing the denotation of the word *physic* through Middle English back to Latin, we discover that *physic* signifies not only natural science but the healing art of medicine as well. I propose that "Father and Son," the concluding story of *Ways of White Folks* (1934), enacts a physics of genius. The quality is the creative principle that enters human history in order to transform it. While this genius is indeed a form of energy, it is energy *willed*. Sometimes its form is liquid, like the blood of violent history and murder that flows. But more important, genius has the characteristic of an artistic self-consciousness that determines its flow. Genius, in this instance, is a biological and creative compulsion to speak across empty spaces and provoke our forebears to answer inquiries about our belonging and our destiny. "Father and Son" is really about the nice complements of figurative and literal change in the world. The fiction depicts the way that the debate over the change by father and son explores which one of the two will indeed control the physical properties of language and, hence, the definitions of humanity.

At the risk of an overly biographical reading, Hughes's life provides a few clues to the persistent recurrence of physics in his subtexts. First of all, his father had insisted during the early twenties that the younger Hughes, then a carefree student at Columbia University, become an engineer.[3] Indeed, the poet would eventually write out vicariously the father's demand for him to be a kind of scientist. Perhaps Langston Hughes, the son, was always answering James Hughes, the father. The poet was proposing that he was, as his kind, the unacknowledged legislator of the world.

Second, the graduation by Langston Hughes from Lincoln University in 1929 had so brilliantly lyricized the distinction between the physical and spiritual realms. For a senior survey

Hughes had researched the way that most black students at Lincoln had preferred to be taught by white professors. A famous old graduate of the institution, while objecting to the nakedness of the factual presentation, had cautioned: "You don't get things out of white folks that way" (310). When the poet had dissented, the elder had asserted that the writer would eventually understand once he was "out of college awhile." The predecessor "crosses" the landscape, the mirror image of the poet's own torment, just as the dreamer faces the physical world. Having never contemplated the demands for compromise, the writer wonders: "For bread how much of the spirit must one give away?" (310). The autobiographer searches for answers through the signs of nineteenth-century abolitionism: "I began to think back to Nat Turner, Harriet Tubman, Sojourner Truth, John Brown, Fred Douglass—*folks* [my italics] who left no *buildings* behind them— only a *wind of words* fanning *the bright flame of the spirit* down the *dark lanes of time*" (310).

Bert Lewis, the mulatto son of Colonel Thomas Norwood and Cora Lewis, a black sharecropper, returns home in "Father and Son" for the summer from the Institute, a run-down boarding school for blacks during the early thirties.[4] When the protagonist was a young boy, the Colonel had made a habit of physically abusing him, often knocking the son beneath the feet of horses on the grounds. The son grows up to violate the manners and customs prescribed for blacks, hence disrupting the established place for them within the hierarchy of power. His father forbids him to go back to school in Atlanta after the summer recess. During a brief encounter in the local post office, a clerk gives Bert twelve cents of change, too little for the purchase of eight three-cent stamps. Bert objects to the mistake on her part, prompting a hostile reaction by whites in the town. Mr. Higgins, a friend of the Colonel, phones the plantation to report the presumably disgusting expression of self-determination by Bert. In the following confrontation at home, Bert strangles his white father and shoots himself at night before a mob can lynch him. But the vigilantes, deprived of their pleasure, string up Willie Lewis, Bert's older brother by eight years.[5] Ironically, the Colonel leaves "no heirs" because all of his illegitimate offspring are black.

To read more deeply, "Bert arrives, at once the most beautiful . . . brightest . . . and badest son." The Colonel retreats to the
library (knowledge, writing) to consult with books of both a
"literary" and "business" nature. Through three different view-
points of consciousness (by Colonel, Bert, and Cora) we hear the
echoed child abuse of the father who knocked the son beneath
the feet of the horses, emblems of id and masculine power. We
see the greeting of the father by the son at evening, the time of
the setting sun, in a diurnal foreshadowing of death. Hence, the
fiction presents specifically the end for Bert, the son of Norwood,
and universally the Son of Man. What makes for the skillful
structure is first the prophesy of change by the lyrical narrator
and then the coming of change in the form of the disowned son.
One subplot takes up the process of explosive change—exciting
leaps forward in the experimentation of the imagination—and a
complementary subplot confines itself to a rather furious debate
about money. The hidden evil in the story is capitalistic greed.

The physics of change voices itself against the silent en-
emy. The moment of prophecy achieves the majestic grandeur of
great elegy while the storyteller celebrates those geniuses who
energize the world. When they have passed from history, "You
feel sick and lonesome and meaningless." Though the teller prepares his reader for the subsequent narrative about a sharecropper's son, the type implies the tragic poet. The rhetorical question, punctuated by parallelism, slows the directness:

> In the chemistry lab at school, did you ever hold a test
> tube, pouring in liquids and powders and seeing nothing
> happen until a *certain* powder is poured in and then every-
> thing begins to smoke and fume, bubble and boil, hiss to
> foam, and sometimes even explode? The tube is suddenly
> full of action and movement and life. Well, there are
> people like those certain liquids or powders; at a given
> moment they come into a room, into a town, even a
> country—and the place is never the same again. Things
> bubble, boil, change. Sometimes the whole world is
> changed. Alexander came. Christ. Marconi. A Russian,
> named Lenin. (220)

Experimentation, in other words, must derive imaginatively
from a flowing concept of life. The revolutionary or artist of bold

innovation, like Bert Lewis, instigates change in the social world, just as a true catalyst sparks transformation in a scientific experiment.

In a way, indeed, each of Hughes's four references was a physicist. Alexander the Great (356 B.C.), king of Macedon (now northeast Greece, southeast Yugoslavia, and southwest Bulgaria), was probably the greatest general of ancient times. By the time he was thirty-two, he had founded an empire ranging from India to the Adriatic Sea. Born the son of King Philip II and Olympia, an Epirote princess, he had a magnetic personality. He was intensely willful and mystical in thought as well as in practical action. A student of Aristotle, he pursued scientific investigations, and he doctored the sick. He looked forward to Jesus Christ, the second figure of the Christian Trinity of God the Father, God the Son, and God the Holy Spirit. Marchese Guglielmo Marconi (b. Bologna, Italy, April 25, 1874; d. Rome, July 20, 1937) refers to the specialization of physics more directly. As the son of Giuseppe Marconi, a successful businessman (as was James Hughes, Langston's father), and Annie Jameson, the youngest daughter of Andrew Jameson of Ireland, Marchese studied at home during his early years. Later at Leghorn, Italy, he deliberated about physics under the direction of Professor Vencenzo Rosa. Marconi also met with Professor Augusto Righi who was, at the University of Bologna, a pioneer in the research of electromagnetic waves.

Though Marconi was never officially a student at any university, in 1894 he browsed a journal containing an article about experiments by Heinrich Hertz on electronic waves. Inspired to try Hertzian concepts for the purposes of communication, Marconi returned home to Pontecchio to test his theory. During several months in 1895 (the year of Booker T. Washington's speech of racial accommodation in Atlanta, Georgia), Marconi completed his apparatus, transmitting signals through the air from one end of his house to the other. Then he did the same again from the house to the garden. Marconi, who in 1909 would share the Nobel Prize for Physics with Ferdinand Braun of Germany, helped usher in the age of wireless telegraphy. He was, in other words, the founder of radio, and he prophesied the emergence of television.

Whatever the differences, each of the four men had a quality of genius. Vladimir Ilich Lenin (b. Simrisk [now Ulyanovsk]
Russia, April 22, 1870; d. Gorki, near Moscow, January 21, 1924),
for example, had been the Russian thinker whose activities had
proved instrumental in the revolution of 1917. While Lenin was a
less talented writer and speaker than was his colleague, Leon
Trotsky (1870–1940), Lenin had a genius that enabled him to
withstand temporary setbacks. Indeed, Lenin held to the ideals
and goals that once laid the foundations of Soviet totalitarianism.
While Lenin had intended to liberate humanity from various
forms of oppression, he had assisted really in shaping these very
limitations in other ways.

Taken together the references are sometimes ironic and
even contradictory. Alexander, the doctor and charismatic
leader, was a conquering soldier; Christ proposed that the meek
were blessed, so they would inherit the earth; Marconi abused
the genius of his talent by helping his native homeland, guided
by the fascist Benito Mussolini, during World War II; Lenin was
certainly a fashionable name to the proletarian Left in the America of the thirties, though his dream brought about the murder of
thousands. Even Bert makes the mistake of thinking that he de-
serves his rights because he is Norwood's bastard son, but the
real reason is that he is a human being. So it is that Bert's presence disrupts the revival that Norwood arranges in order to re-
store the status quo on the plantation. Hence, blacks are "not
quite the same as they had been in the morning. And never to be
the same again."

To return to the inciting moment at the post office, the
sales clerk does not expect to argue with African Americans. Bert
keeps to his principles, "holding out the incorrect change." She
becomes quite irritated while "counting the change." Now seeing the "change," she recognizes the error. But, observing the
bluish grey eyes on a black man, she screams. She resents the
signs of his educated privilege. As her head falls forward in the
manner of the violated Southern belle, two or three white men
attempt to remove Bert from line. While striking out at the
whites to give one of them a bloody mouth, rather awkwardly,
Bert "remembers" once he had been a football *player*. Then the
female clerk screams again. The melodrama, in other words,

waxes too high, the hysteria suggesting a stigma of gender. Finally, she "recovers" to narrate the tale: "Oh, my God! it was terrible." Why the delay? For a fleeting moment, I believe, she thinks about changing her Southern world. She faces, in other words, the same dilemma as Bert, though her psychic energy releases itself negatively (228).

While Norwood calls for the continued *narrative* of the status quo, Bert and Cora respond with the *narrating* of change. Even as the story proceeds, the tale prepares to finish, "The day that ends our story." So for now the notepad is cleared for a new story of American race relations to be written. Near the end, Thomas Norwood must exit his library—the emblem of learning, arts, and business—to yell his disgust at Sam, the house black. Almost hopelessly, the father brandishes a stick at Bert, who lunges in the family Ford down the road. By now the burning, blazing summer has supplanted the cool water in which Cora has washed plums. The earth, so "flooded" with the early heat of autumn, "shimmers" to prepare for the eventual flow of Norwood's blood. The Colonel, with a pistol from his open drawer, faces the waning of his own sexual power "strengthless and limp."

After Bert shoots himself, thereby depriving the mob of the presumed delight of lynching him, Cora addresses the dead Colonel, whose body lies prostrate on the floor before her. As she pulls the body feverishly, Talbot bursts in upon the scene. When he has Jim, a friend, call in to town in order to arrange for a posse, Cora realizes that "night had come." In a soliloquy with the dead Colonel, she bids him to rise, reminding him of all the occasions for which she served him well in bed, and demanding recompense now in the form of her son's life. From far off in the distance, she hears the hounds pursuing Bert while the body at her feet remains now unmoving. Finally, she goes upstairs in the mansion and leaves the Colonel's corpse lying on the floor for a long time. While she continues to hear the barking of the hounds, she prepares a hiding place in the attic for Bert, who she knows will come home to die. When Cora says "night had come," the statement extends to the metaphysical universe.

Cora speaks of "my boy" or "our boy" fleeing the lyncher's rope. But the Colonel talks about Cora's children, Cora's child, and the boy. She asks Bert to enact a law of physics—to run—as an expression of genetic bonding as true as running water. By the time of his flight back from the outside world, once the mob has cut him off from the swamp, he finishes orgasmically—"coming back" to his "father's house." Hence, he has completed the brilliant word acrostic[6] that the omniscient narrator began:

> "Lawd, chile, Bert's come home . . ."
> "Lawd, chile, and he said . . ."
> "Lawd, chile, he said . . ."
> "Lawd, chile . . ."
> "Lawd . . ."

An acrostic, literally a stairway, makes sense when read vertically from any angle. The 119th Psalm, the stanzas of which are arranged according to the Hebrew alphabet, is the earliest known illustration of the kind. Historically, the acrostic means a written composition, typically a poem, in which the various letters of lines can be read to spell out different words from those of the literal denotation. Verses of religion and love poems appeared in Europe for many years until the last century, during which time the form became unfashionable. Indeed, perhaps much of the boring literalness of twentieth-century discourse can be explained by the death of the acrostic, resisting stubbornly the idea that we can ever reduce human existence to scientific writing, to the narrow confines of linear space. Today the design of the acrostic appears most often in word puzzles. Perhaps one of the best-known is the *Double-Crostic*, by Elizabeth S. Kingsley, published in the *Saturday Review* for 1934.

Once read from the left corner at the top, then to the right at the bottom, the verbal graphic of Hughes's narrator in "Father and Son" ends in despair, "Lawd . . ." the expression, in the descent from the left corner at the bottom, then straight on up to the top, reveals an equal despair for the acknowledged God from whom no explanation will come: "Lawd . . . Lawd." When the descent leads downward, from the top of the second column to the bottom, an equally tragic wail sounds through human generations, "chile . . ./chile . . ." As with the fall implied in the second column, the folk regression in the third one ends in tragic nothingness, "Bert's/and/he said. . . ." Only the pattern from the far right corner to the far left one, then from the bottom left corner to the top right, promises Judaeo-Christian redemption: "Come home . . ./he said /he said /he said /Lawd, chile/Lawd, chile . . ./Lawd/" "Lawd . . ./chile . . . he said . . ./and he said . . ./come home. . . ." From the hum in the quarters, the voices have expanded to the totality of God with the wave effects of radio and the telegraphy of change. Already the narrator has told us that Jesus hadn't borne the cross so well since World War I. What he means was that so many African Americans had died to make the world safe for democracy they wanted the elusive freedom that had seemed to go up in smoke. Was it the red summer of 1919 that the Colonel had remembered one day when seeing his son "coming back from the river"?

At once Langston Hughes achieves in "Father and Son" the grandeur of lyric and the subtle understatement of great fiction. The rare fusion signifies genius shaping itself through words. No doubt Bert exudes in more violent fashion the same quiet energy that the character Berry, the signature[7] of Langston Hughes, exemplifies in a tale about crippled children. Elsewhere, Roy Williams, a gifted violinist, comes "home" to die in a story by that title.[8] In "Ask Your Mama" (1961), the poetic cantor asserts, "Come what may Langston Hughes" (41–42). By 1965, only two years before the writer's death, the storyteller brings genius down to earth once more. Lynn Clarisse, a fiction in a Semple tale, abandons gaiety in a New York cafe—a clean, well-lighted place—to return to the sit-ins of the South. Indeed, even Semple himself, a medium of laughter for over twenty years, has fallen silent, scarred by the urgency of the times.[9] Almost always the poetic gift of Langston Hughes has remarkable resilience in the face of change. In time, Hughes believed, the human spirit would prevail. Once more it would take shape as the physics of his Dream.

NOTES

1. Other variants of the same theme include *Mulatto,* the play that was completed in draft by 1930, though it was only produced on Broadway in 1935, and "The Barrier," an unpublished libretto. *See* Sybil Ray Ricks, "A Textual Comparison of Langston Hughes' *Mulatto,* 'Father and Son,' and 'The Barrier,'" *Black American Literature Forum* 15 (Fall 1981): 101–103; David Michael Nifong, "Narrative Technique and Theory in *The Ways of White Folks," Black American Literature Forum* 15 (Fall 1981): 93–96; R. Baxter Miller, *The Art and Imagination of Langston Hughes* (Lexington: University Press of Kentucky, 1989), 104–109; Richard K. Barksdale, *Praisesong of Survival* (Urbana: University of Illinois Press, 1992). The standard biographies are Faith Berry, *Langston Hughes: Before and Beyond Harlem* (Westport, CT: Lawrence Hill, 1983); Arnold Rampersad, *The Life of Langston Hughes,* 2 vols. (New York: Oxford University Press, 1986, 1988).

2. Langston Hughes, "Harlem," *Selected Poems* (New York: Vintage Books, 1959, 1974), 268.

3. Langston Hughes, *The Big Sea* (New York: Knopf, 1940; Hill & Wang, 1986).

4. Actually, the feel of the story seems to be much more that of the period of Reconstruction following the Civil War that had taken place between April 12, 1861, through April 9, 1865.

5. The eldest, Bertha, had traveled north with the Jubilee Singers, suggesting Fisk University though she supposedly went to school in Atlanta as well, and remained in Chicago; Sailie, the youngest and Bert's junior by three years, returned to college in Atlanta.

6. *See also* James Emanuel, "The Literary Experiments of Langston Hughes," *CLA Journal* 11 (June 1967): 335–344.

7. Hughes dedicates the volume to his California Patron, Noel Sullivan: "The ways of white folks,/I mean some white folks . . ." [signed] BERRY.

8. *Ways of White Folks,* respectively, 32–48, 171–812.

9. Richard K. Barksdale, "Comic Relief in Langston Hughes' Poetry," *Black American Literature Forum* 15 (Fall 1981): 108–111.

The Girl with the Red Dress On

Kristin Hunter-Lattany
University of Pennsylvania

> See the girl with the red dress on.
> She can do the Birdland all night long . . .
>
> —Ray Charles, *What'd I Say?*

I wore a red hat and blouse with my sober navy suit to moderate the fiction panel of the Lincoln University conference on "Langston Hughes: The Man and the Writer." I wore these red accessories in honor of the man who wrote, in "Wake": "Tell all my mourners/To mourn in red/Cause there ain't no sense/In my bein' dead" (*Selected Poems of Langston Hughes*, 39).

But what I really wanted to wear that day, and searched for in vain in my closet, was an honest-to-goodness Red Dress—the kind of Red Dress that goodness has absolutely nothing to do with—and a pair of red hussy shoes to match. The man whose life and work we were celebrating that day would have appreciated such an outfit. But, to be honest, it takes a special kind of attitude to wear The Red Dress—a brazen, provocative, who-cares attitude, which I did not possess—or I would have owned The Dress. I think, though, that this special attitude was possessed by Hughes himself and by some of his favorite characters.

Hughes described the Red Dress in the wonderful first novel he wrote at Lincoln, *Not Without Laughter*. It was worn by Harriett, the protagonist's younger aunt, in the triumphant scene of her performance as "Princess of the Blues":

> Harriett entered in a dress of glowing orange, flame-like
> against the ebony of her skin, barbaric, yet beautiful as a
> jungle princess. She swayed toward the footlights, while
> Billy teased the keys of the piano into a hesitating delicate
> jazz. Then she began to croon a new song—a popular ver-
> sion of an old Negro melody, refashioned with words
> from Broadway." (297)

Yes, the adjective is "orange," but in every sense, this is
The Red Dress—and Harriett was, if not the original Girl with
the Red Dress On, an exceedingly elegant and spirited successor.
That she is Hughes's favorite character in the novel—that she is,
in fact, the author's alter ego and sassy spokesperson—cannot be
doubted. Every other character in the novel is flawed—Tempy
by her bourgeois pride; Annjee by her limited aspirations; Jimboy by laziness; and even Hager by too much Christian acceptance and forgiveness. Only Harriett meets the author's ideals of
talent, spirited self-esteem, and refusal to accept second-class
status.

And, in addition to wearing the Red Dress, Harriett, like
her author, waves the red flag of defiance at church, state, and
the status quo of bourgeois blacks and oppressive whites, especially when they are exalted by her pious mother, Hager. Here is
Harriett's response to Hager's comment about how well, com-
pared to Harriett, her sister Tempy is doing:

> "So respectable you can't touch her with a ten-foot pole,
> that's Tempy! Annjee's all right . . . but don't tell me about
> Tempy. Just because she's married a mailclerk with a little
> property, she won't even see her family any more. When
> niggers get up in the world, they act just like white folks—
> don't pay you no mind. And Tempy's that kind of nig-
> ger—she's up in the world now!" (*Not Without Laughter*,
> 41)

For another example of Hughes's opinion of Negroes with
bourgeois pretensions, here is Mrs. Angelina Walls's fight-insti-
gating scene from "Slice Him Down":

> Mrs. Walls explained, "The floor at this club's too full of
> riff-raff for me . . . I come here to Reno on a *train*, myself."
> She was aiming directly at Charlie-Mae sitting beside her.

"That's more'n your boy friend did," said Sling, grinning at Terry.

"Well, if he didn't," said Mrs. Walls in a high half-drunken voice, "he's a real man right on. He earns a decent living shining shoes—not working down in no Chinese rat hole like you, cleaning up after gamblers, and running around with womens what don't know they name."

Sling was shamed into silence—but Charlie-Mae whirled around toward Mrs. Walls and slapped her face. Angelina's beer went all over her dress.

. . . "Terry, protect me," Mrs. Walls cried, holding her well-slapped cheek. "A decent girl can't live in this town." (*Something in Common*, 88)

Harriett's next retort, to Hager's pronouncement that her wish to have a good time "ain't right, and ain't Christian," challenges Christendom as fiercely as did Hughes's later poem, "Goodbye Christ" (1941), which caused him so much trouble in mid-career:

. . . Goodbye,
Christ Jesus Lord God Jehova,
Beat it on away from here now.
Make way for a new guy with no religion at all—
A real guy named
Marx Communist Lenin Peasant Stalin Worker ME

I said, ME! . . . (Rampersad, II, 4)

No African American author before Hughes dared to challenge Christianity so explicitly, and no one has since, except, possibly, Ishmael Reed in *Mumbo Jumbo*. But Harriett's flaming and inflammatory speech waves as red, if not as Red, a flag in the face of Christendom as does "Goodbye Christ" eleven years later. And Harriett has even more blasphemous things to say:

" 'Aw, the church has made a lot of you old Negroes act like Salvation Army people.' The girl returned, throwing the dried knives and forks on the table. 'Afraid to even laugh on Sundays, afraid for a girl and boy to look at one another, or for people to go to dances. Your old Jesus is white, I guess, that's why! He's white and stiff and don't like niggers!" (NWL, 42)

Harriett's characterization of Jesus anticipates Ishmael Reed's characterization of the stiff white Christian Atonist Order in *Mumbo Jumbo*, as a grim death cult who want to destroy everyone who can dance—because they can't.

Harriett goes on:

> . . . disregarding her mother's pain. "Look at Tempy, the highest-class Christian in the family—Episcopal, and so holy she can't even visit her own mother. Seems like all the good-time people are bad, and all the old Uncle Toms and mean, dried-up, long-faced niggers fill the churches. I don't never intend to join a church if I can help it!" (NWL, 42)

It might have been the times—the lean, left-leaning thirties, as opposed to the patriotic wartime of 1941, when "Goodbye Christ" met with such vitriolic objections—or it might have been the protective disguise of fiction, but Hughes got away with putting sentiments in the mouth of a sassy teenage girl that he later found he could not express directly in his poetry, at least not without grave repercussions to his career. The poem "Goodbye Christ" caused "a squall of controversy with Langston Hughes at its center" and such a hostile public scrutiny of his basic beliefs and intentions that Hughes felt compelled to repudiate it "as a regrettable error of his immature youth" (Rampersad, II, 4).

No such embarrassment afflicts Harriett, youth, immaturity and all. Rebuked by Hager for "Runnin' de streets and wearin' red (!) silk stockings!" (*Not Without Laughter*, 43) and exhorted to "be good, honey, and follow Jesus . . ." (45), she calls her mother "You old Christian fool!" and gets away with it—in fact, she gets to walk out of the house and into a waiting car, which her nephew Sandy watches until it becomes "a red taillight in the summer dusk" (45). Red silk stockings, red-hot words, red lights, and, above all, The Red Dress combine to keep Harriett aflame in the reader's imagination.

There can be no doubt that Hughes's sentiments and Harriett's were the same. Harriett got away with expressing hers because her timing was better, that's all (she spoke out in 1930, not in 1941), or because fiction was safer.

The Girl With the Red Dress On also has her say about White Folks in the chapter of *Not Without Laughter* with that title. In flaming, flaying words, she anticipates the worker-allied, Soviet-sympathizing, class-struggling Hughes of later years—and again gets away with it:

> ". . . I ain't never been South . . . but I know 'em right here . . . and I hate 'em!"
>
> "De Lawd hears you," said Hagar.
>
> 'I don't care if He does hear me, Mama! You and Annjee are too easy. You just take whatever white folks give you—*coon* to your face, and *nigger* behind your backs—and don't say nothing. You run to some white person's back door for every job you get, and then they pay you one dollar for every five dollars' worth of work, and fire you whenever you get ready." (74)

For evidence that Harriett's ideas are the same as Hughes's, the reader has only to compare the above speech to "Porter":

> I must say
> Yes, sir,
> To you all the time.
> Yes, sir!
> Yes, sir!
> All my days
> Climbing up a great big mountain
> Of yes, sirs!
>
> Rich old white man
> Owns the world.
> Gimme yo' shoes
> To shine.
>
> Yes, sir! (*Selected Poems*, 169)

Just in case anybody mistakes her message, Harriett has the last word on White Folks at the end of that chapter:

> "They wouldn't have a single one of us around if they could help it. It don't matter to them if we're shut out of a

job. It don't matter to them if niggers have only the back
row at the movies. It don't matter to them when they hurt
our feelings without caring and treat us like slaves down
South and like beggars up North. No, it don't matter to
them. White folks run the world, and the only thing colored folks are expected to do is work and grin and take off
their hats as if it don't matter . . . O, I hate 'em!'" (NWL,
78)

—Words so red-hot that if water were poured on them,
they would sizzle. Honest, angry words from the mouth of a
teenage Girl with the Red Dress On. They went unpunished by
the critics and unattacked by the conservatives who would not
let their author say the same things himself a few years later. But,
in the person of Sandy, he thought them:

> Buster was going to pass for white when he left Stanton.
> "I don't blame him," thought Sandy. "Sometimes I hate
> white people too, like Aunt Harriet used to say she did."

> He understood then why many old Negroes said, "Take
> all this world and give me Jesus!" It was because they
> couldn't get this world anyway—it belonged to the white
> folks. They alone had the power to give or withhold at
> their back doors. Always back doors. . . . (NWL, 162)

And, eleven years later, Hughes wrote:

Southern Mammy Sings (1941)

Not meanin' to be sassy
And not meanin' to be smart—
But sometimes I think that white folks
Just ain't got no heart.
No, ma'am!
Just ain't got no heart.
(*Selected Poems*, p. 162)

Like all the Girls With the Red Dress On, Harriett is in for
some rough times after she lands—where else? in the red-light
district of Stanton, Kansas, called The Bottoms. But, according to
Hughes, the Bottoms was not such a bad place:

> It was a gay place—people did what they wanted to, or
> what they had to do, and didn't care—for in the Bottoms
> folks ceased to struggle against the boundaries between

good or bad, or white and black, and surrendered amiably
to immorality. Beyond Pearl Street, across the tracks, people of all colors came together for the sake of joy" (NWL,
216)

And if the reader wonders briefly how Harriett handles
her hatred of white folks in this place of joyous interrracial min-
gling—and never finds out—still, we recognize the Bottoms as
the place where all pretensions are dropped and all false moral-
ity abandoned, greatly benefiting the brotherhood of man. The
Bottoms sound a bit like the Soviet Union in the Thirties, but
mainly they are Hughes's favorite U.S. haunts, oases of pleasure
forever inhabited by Zora Neale Hurston's "Negroes farthest
down" and a bevy of Girls in Red Dresses. Clearly, Hughes loves
the Bottoms. But he loves Harriett too much to let her stay there.
No, little Harriett in her Red Dress is headed straight for the Top.

After Hager dies, Sandy's respectable Aunt Tempy proves
generous, but too strict and narrow for Sandy's temperament.
Tempy despises spirituals, the blues, and Booker T. Washington
but admires opera and everything else white and "refined,"
which leaves out Sandy, his girlfriend Pansetta—and even his
grandmother Hager, Tempy's mother.

> Tempy thought of her mother then and wished that
> black Aunt Hager had not always worn her apron in the
> streets, uptown and everywhere! Of course, it was clean
> and white and seemed to suit the old lady, but aprons
> weren't worn by the best people. When Tempy was in the
> hospital for an operation shortly after her marriage, they
> wouldn't let Hager enter by the front door—and Tempy
> never knew whether it was on account of her color or the
> apron! (NWL, 241)

And, when he joins her in Chicago, Sandy's mother An-
jee's limited horizons impel her to urge her son to stay out of
school and work to "help" her.

But Harriett, the heroine of the novel, saves the day. Wearing the Red Dress and singing the blues, always a winning combination, have paid off—she is a star performer at a State Street
theater. She also has the values instilled in her by her mother.
Though she, herself, did not finish school, she is horrified by her
sister's plans for Sandy to stop:

"Why, Aunt Hager'd turn over in her grave if she heard
you talking so calmly about Sandy leaving school—the
way she wanted to make something out of this kid."
(NWL, 302)

Then Harriett comes through handsomely, by offering to
replace Sandy's earnings so that he can go to school—and to buy
his books, too. The Girl with the Red Dress On emerges as the
novel's triumphant hero: she is a successful star who supports
the best values of her family and the highest aspirations of the
race—and not just with words, but with cash.

There are other Girls with the Red Dress On in Hughes's
fiction—Charlie-Mae in "Slice Him Down" comes to mind, as
does Zarita in the "Simple" series—and all of them are memorable. But—perhaps because their author, while always san-
guine, inevitably became less naive—none are as totally admirable or as successful, both as characters and in the worldly
sense, as Langston Hughes's first Girl With the Red Dress On—
Sandy's adorable aunt, Harriett Rogers.

Works Cited

Hughes, Langston. *Not Without Laughter.* New York: Macmillan, 1930,
      1969.

———. *Something in Common and Other Stories.* New York: Hill & Wang,
      1963. (Originally published in *Laughing to Keep from Crying.* New
      York: Henry Holt, 1955.)

———. *Selected Poems of Langston Hughes.* New York: Alfred A. Knopf,
      1959.

Rampersad, Arnold. *The Life of Langston Hughes, Volume II: 1941–1967. I
      Dream a World.* New York: Oxford University Press, 1988.

Reading the Woman's Face in Langston Hughes and Roy DeCarava's *Sweet Flypaper of Life*

Thadious M. Davis

Brown University

The Sweet Flypaper of Life, Langston Hughes's 1955 collaboration with photographer Roy DeCarava, has not received critical attention, though it was, as Arnold Rampersad points out, one of his critical successes: "No book by Hughes was ever greeted so rhapsodically." It was acclaimed as "its own kind of art"; "a delicate and lovely fiction-document"; "astonishing verisimilitude" (II, 249). The small, cheaply printed, yet beautiful book is somewhat of an anomaly in the scholarship on Hughes's fiction.

In examining the small volume, I have been struck by its similarity to an earlier effort *Twelve Million Black Voices* (1941) by Richard Wright with photographic direction by Edwin Rosskam. The conjunction of visual representation of the lives of African Americans with literary text is another way of bringing art into the lives of ordinary people, of showing the faces of the people within the contexts of daily experience, and of telling the stories of their human relationships in counterdistinction to the stereotypical constructions of their lives. In an introduction to the Thunder's Mouth Press edition of *Twelve Million Black Voices* (1988), David Bradley remarks the "lyrical power" of Wright's text, "an impressionistic rather than logical structure. . . . a fluid power of a clarity of expression that [Wright] would not achieve again until the mid-fifties" (xvi–xvii).

While Wright's effort is a racial history, Hughes's is a communal history; the difference between the story told by an observer, external thought clearly empathetic and identified with the subject, and the story told by a participant whose observations begin with the immediate, the sensory accessible, and by extension involve the larger whole. And though Wright may have figured himself into the faces within the photographs, and into the racialized "we" subjectifying his narrative, he also abstracts himself from the historicizing process as his foreword to *Twelve Million Black Voices* implies:

> This text assumes that those few Negroes who have lifted themselves . . . above the lives of their fellow-blacks—like single fishes that leap and flash for a split second above the surface of the sea—are but fleeting exceptions to that vast, tragic school that swims below in the depth, against the current, silently and heavily, struggling against the waves of vicissitudes that spell a common fate. It is not, however, to celebrate or exalt the plight of humble folk who swim in the depths that I select the conditions of their lives as examples of normality, but rather to seize upon that which is qualitative and abiding in Negro experience, to place within full and constant view the collective humanity whose triumphs and defeats are shared by the majority, whose gains in security mark an advance in the level of consciousness attained by the broad masses in their costly and tortuous upstream journey. (xix–xx)

Hughes's text, on the other hand, collapses the authorial identity into the autobiographical construction of one Mary Bradley. The distinction between fiction, history, and autobiography are intentionally blurred, and Hughes's own autobiography is transfigured into the fictional Mary Bradley's historicizing her life within contemporary Harlem. Hughes's project is fiction, then, in a way that Wright's is not. The cite of narrative reality is the invented subject, Mary Bradley, who initially enters the text as voice and vision and who on the final page leaves as image and reality.

Written in the voice of Sister Mary Bradley, 113 West 134th Street, New York City, *The Sweet Flypaper of Life* takes as its project the fitting of narrative to images. In a stream of conscious-ness provoked by a brush with death, the "bicycle of the Lord bearing His messenger," sister Mary talks through the reasons why she cannot acquiesce to the call: "'Boy, take that wire right on back to St. Peter because I am not prepared to go. I might be a little sick, but as yet I ain't no ways tired'" (7). Humorous and poignant, she is unprepared to untangle herself from the living, from family ("'I got to look after Ronnie Belle. . . .'"), from race ("'I want to stay here and see what this integration the Supreme Court has done decreed is going to be like'") (7). In refusing to sign her name to the telegram, she not only puts death in abeyance, but she also initiates the process of articulating an identity beyond a single textual referent.

The construction of Mary Bradley's social, familial, cul-tural contexts is both an act of memory and an act of invention. It is, too, an instance of what R. Baxter Miller labels in *The Art and Imagination of Langston Hughes* (1989), Hughes's "task of record-ing cultural history," in which "the autobiographical imagination . . . expresses the bond between history and self as well as that between fact and interpretation" (121). In *Sweet Flypaper,* Hughes displaces his own signature with the photograph of Mary Bradley, signed on the last page of the text: "Here I am" (96). The signing of the text in the end as hers—that is, female, mother, grandmother, elderly, African American, urban, struggling, surviving, loving, and smiling from under the brim of her best hat and looking directly into the camera while holding on to an iron fence—also displaces the shaping act of DeCarava, the photographer. Mary Bradley's reality becomes the subject of her own iconography or subjectivity, not of Hughes's autograph or of DeCarava's camera. While she does not author or photograph herself, she does narrate, tell, portray, and render events and people and the emotions connecting the two within a spatial context that is at once the Harlem she describes, and therefore in-vents, and the photographs she issues from. At the end, she stands, seemingly larger in size than any of the other photo-graphic images, though there is no difference in the actual di-mensions.

The "image of the Black woman," according to Miller, "signified the rise and fall of [Hughes's] literary imagination.

What made the Black woman central to Hughes's world was her role as griot and keeper of memories. . . . she sought to keep alive the rites that facilitated the passage from slavery to freedom. Here was often the lyrical imagination. . . . a rite of celebration shared with the audience" (121). Miller's observation seems applicable to Hughes in his creative interaction with the voice of the elderly African American female, Mary Bradley, a personae and a projection, emanating from Hughes's observation of and empathy with older women of color. However, his interaction with Mary Bradley's voice is an impersonal, and yet completely personal, projection of his own experiences, vocalized in his participation in the lives of Harlemites from an unthreatening female, grandmotherly locus of being.

Ultimately pragmatic, Hughes's writing unifies the speech act with its visual framing texts, the photographs of DeCarava, a painter and photographer by training. While on a Guggenheim Fellowship in 1952, DeCarava angled his camera on the Harlem community and completed over 2,000 photographs which, until he contacted Hughes, simply sat on a shelf (Rampersad, II, 242). After seeing a selection of about 300, Hughes responded immediately: "We have to get these published!" (Rampersad, II, 242–243). DeCarava's photographs struck a personal chord evoking Hughes's own connections to Harlem life; Rampersad reveals that within days of the meeting with DeCarava, Hughes put a group of the photographs in his study "as inspiration," and started writing, almost nonstop, his second autobiography, *I Wonder as I Wander* (II, 242). The urgency of that writing, certainly nothing new for Hughes, who in the mid-1950s was churning out historical books as fast as he could to keep the "wolf from his door," the urgency, however, suggests the power of DeCarava's visual images to galvanize Hughes into a self-reflective mode.

The dual communicative nature of the enterprise aims at both a verbally oriented access and a visually oriented one. The sentences, strung across the pages, introduce and depart from the photographic images. The conjoined effort is a performance of communication as the stored and restored contextual realities of both the individual behind the camera and the individual behind the word. The impact is an emotional, sensory, and intellectual response to the linked representation of the photographer and the writer.

Invited into the text by images that are both photographic and linguistic, a reader is invited to become not a voyeur, but a witness who can comprehend what is at stake in the representations, yet nonetheless a spectator who can envision a whole through the immediacy of its graphic parts. While no political agenda is immediately available in the photographs, the visualization of African Americans in an urban setting captures a variety of experiences with the constancy of color. The subjects are black, within a world uniformly black, and so the corresponding discursive texture. Contained, framed, but valued and respected, the photographic subjects are not posed in attitude or restricted in motion; the photographer allows the subjects their own expression and their own beauty, their own pain.

To narrate from Sister Mary's perspective is to assume an angle of vision encompassing generations and transformations. It absorbs and suppresses the self even while recapitulating the obsessions of self. The combination of an intergenerational lens with a sharp focus on change at once allows the telling to assert its own significance as continuity and to insist on its own place in the process, in the effecting of change. The interpretative imagination Sister Mary displays foregrounds the necessity of priorities, or ordering one's life, and thus a hierarchical significance of generations and transformations emerges from Sister Mary's interpretive ordering, which places self at the center but, at the same time, at the lower end of priorities. In prioritizing her grandchildren, especially Rodney, and her children, particularly her youngest daughter Melinda, and her community, and only then herself, Sister Mary orders a world that could otherwise seem chaotic, without pattern.

The written communication, however, is markedly political. It argues for the possibility of a better life, within the "sweet flypaper," within the lived and varied experiences of the subjects. The sameness of the language, dovetailed to the pictures, is the sameness of difference. The argument hinges upon comprehension of the momentous possibility of the Supreme Court's striking down of "separate but equal"; on the ever-present potential of Rodney and the children of Mary's offspring; on the people-driven activities of "Picket lines picketing" (79); "And at night the street meetings on the corner—" (80); "talking about 'Buy black'" (81); "'Africa for the Africans'" (82); "and 'Ethiopia shall stretch forth her hand'" (83), and in all the voice of racial reality: "And some joker in the crowd always says, 'And draw back a nub!'" (83). In this sequence Hughes writes into the photographs the undercurrent of emergent political expression and a sense of the static disappointment already always interpolated into any racially aware present.

Without despair and without bitterness, the voice inscribes at once the slyly veiled, politically subdued, writerly Hughes, distrusting established institutions but unwilling to dismiss the agency of grassroots efforts; and the voice inscribes the articulate folk speaker Mary Bradley, the unseen yet iconic maternal presence, whose personal politics is staunchly based on uncompromising love and direct intervention and faith in coalitions of whoever shares her beliefs and participates in her fight, as the exchange between Miss Mary and the janitor suggests: "'Miss Mary, I hear tell you's down—but with no intentions of going out'" (91). "I says: 'You're right! I done got my feet caught in the sweet flypaper of life—and I'll be dogged if I want to get loose'" (92). Life metaphorically is both sweet and entrapping; death is its logical, inescapable outcome, yet an outcome mediated by the sensory pleasure of sweetness.

The brief unregulated survey of a community through the multi-faceted members of Sister Mary's family positions the class stratification becoming more pronounced on the eve of integration in the mid-1950s at the center of a discourse on family, familial responsibility, children, parental duty, and the social institutions beginning to fail African American people. Instructive and educative by its very ordering, the narrative patterning deemphasizes a single conventional middle-class paradigm for racial and familial survival. Mary's litany of the "good stock in her family," those following the way of marriage, work, houses, upward mobility, is swift and short, buried a third of the way through her narrative: Chickasaw, Mary's "most up-and-coming grandchild, declares soon as he gets married, he's gonna get [a car] too, so he won't have to ride the bus to work" (20); "I got some fine grandchildren, like my son Fred's three that lives up by the Harlem River" (34); "Or like my daughter Ellen's daughter whose name is Ellen, too" (35); "Oh, there is some good stock in my family. Like Ellen's mother who really takes care of her house. And my middle boy is well married, to a girl who is a real pretty typewriter" (36).

The daughter Melinda with whom Mary lives, Melinda's husband Jerry, and their four children, however, subvert the static objectifying image of "good stock," "fine children." In a sustained development occupying twenty pages and uncharacteristically long in this short text, Melinda's family emerges as functional: four children including a set of twins in five years of marriage, as well as a party every Saturday night (45–46); "can't nobody say when [Jerry's] home he ain't a family man. Crazy about his children—and his children are crazy about him" (51). It is functional yet flawed: "This world is like a crossword puzzle in the *Daily News*" (45); a son who "wants a gun that shoot both ways at once" (58); a father who sometimes forgets to come home (61). It is flawed but central to Mary's recognition of a subjectified unit only partly controlled by her gaze. Not without a hint of irony, Mary prefaces her bittersweet portrait of Melinda's family by observing: "Me, I always been all tangled up in life— which ain't always so sanitary as we might like it to be" (43). Her words signal a correspondence between her own and her daughter's relationship with life.

However, it is not Mary's rendering of Melinda's household but rather her positioning of her grandson Rodney and his slow, easy movement at the beginning of her monologue that serves as a catalyst for the narrative of the unraveling of myths of mobility and of the persistent social constructions of race:

> That Rodney! That street's done got Rodney! How his father and his mother can wash their hands of Rodney, I do not know, when he is the spitting image of them both. But they done put him out, so's they can keep on good-timing themselves, I reckon [photo of man and woman embracing, 10]. So I told him, 'Come here and live with your grandma.' And he come.
>
> Now, Lord, I don't know—why did I want to take Rodney? But since I did, do you reckon my prayers will reach down in all them king-kong basements, and sing with the

juke boxes, and walk in the midnight streets with Rodney?
. . . Because there's something in that boy. You know and I
know there's something in Rodney. If he got lost in his
youthhood, it just might not be his fault, Lord. I were wild
myself when I were young—and to tell the truth, ever so
once in a while, I still feels the urge. But sometimes, I
wonder why the only time that boy moves fast is when
he's dancing. When there's music playing, girls have to
just keep looking to see where he's at, he dances so fast.
Where's he at? Where's he at? [photo of a girl dancing
with head to one side, 11]

Mary's prayer for Rodney is the longest sustained piece of
narrative uninterrupted by photographs in *Sweet Flypaper*. Its en-
coded revelation, however, is that Rodney is beyond the control
of Mary's gaze and that he signals Mary's position as spectator,
though one involved in attempting to construct a logic of Harlem
life out of its images of contradiction. Ambivalently, Mary herself typecasts both the Rodney she sees and his relationship to
music and good times; she acknowledges his faults: "But when
he's talking or listening, or lounging, he just looks sleepy—
drinking beer down in the basement with them boys" (12);
"Rodney has to come up here to me to borrow subway fare to
take [his girlfriend out]" (13); "Had a baby by Sugarlee before he
were even seventeen . . . he did not pay that baby no mind—not
even to walk it like other young fathers do" (27); "Rodney's child
growed up like that little boy down the street, sad. He don't
never smile" (28). But Rodney's fate is not simply the focal point
of disintegration of the family and intergenerational confusion
about courses of corrective action, but also the point of Mary's
narrative strategies for coherence, textual and experiential cohe-
sion, though qualified because as a masculine racial construction
Rodney seems vulnerable to a fetishizing of the ambiguous black
male youth.

Rodney recurs throughout; situated as the entry and the
exit from the communal habits and ethics, behavior and values,
he grounds Mary's function in reflecting life and in resisting
death. At the center of the narrative, and of her reason for living,
is her grandson Rodney. The passage "He never moves fast—not
even to reach his hand out for a dollar—except when he is
dancing. And crazy about music. Can tell you every horn that

ever blowed on every juke-box in the neighborhood" (13) serves
as the entrance to a discourse on the activities of young people
and their differences from Mary's generation in terms of their
tastes in music and their desire for cars, which then leads to
Mary's poignant differentiation between contemporary subway
riders, who are likened to domestic workers—the women of
Mary's generation.

Rodney is a controlling and deflecting trope for the class
difference and the material sameness of conditions in Harlem; he
connects Mary back to her past and poses a complicated argument for her future, both of which by extension signify the
Harlem community: "And then we got Rodney—and he's my
boy [photo of men grouped indoors]. They say in the neighborhood sometimes Rodney can say things that makes everybody
set up and take notice—even if he don't wake up till night. I used
to be a kind of sleepyhead myself, so I understands him" (41).
Her strategy for decoding the mystery of Rodney's difference is
to read the values of her own past into his present. Following a
series of scenes painting what can be seen from the windows of
Harlem's porchless buildings, she concludes:

> Yes, you can sit in your window anywhere in Harlem and
> see plenty. Of course, some windows is better to set in
> than others. . . . But back windows ain't much good for
> looking out. I never did like looking backwards no how. I
> always did believe in looking out front—looking ahead—
> which is why I's worried about Rodney. [photo of young
> man half in shadows, 84]

The looking ahead from front windows is complicated by the
uncertain future not of Mary but of Rodney, the youth with music and dance and ideas moving him only in a nocturnal world
that is at odds not only with the backdrop of the Supreme Court
decision and eminent change, but also with the foreground of the
racially connected and familial responsible community that
Mary produces in visioning Harlem.

What is especially striking is the elegiac tone that contra-
dicts Sister Mary's refusal to answer St. Peter's call. "Some have
been where they are going. And some can't seem to make up
their minds which way to go; And some ain't going no place at
all. . . ." (67–68). "But it's sad if you ain't invited [followed by a

photograph of a lone man facing away from the camera and toward a four-columned entry to a building]. It's too bad there's no
front porches in Harlem [followed by a photograph of an apartment building presenting to a camera two stories and ten windows of its facade]" (70). And the question punctuating all:
"What do you reckon's out there in them streets for that boy?"
(85). The parade of people, "beat up by life," offers no answers:
Mazie (one of Rodney's girlfriends); Ada (another girlfriend
whose life is work and sleep and tiredness and waiting for Rodney); Miss Mary's first husband from Carolina. "He were cut up
by life, too. But it never got him down. I never knowed him to go
to sleep neither" (91). The imposition of change onto life, un-
wanted but inevitable change, is the message of the refused telegram initiating Mary's monologue, and it is the message of her
reiterated statement of entanglement with life which ultimately
figures her death.

The Sweet Flypaper of Life functions as a prelude to change:
the deterioration of Harlem, the emptiness of youth, the passing
of the up-from-the-South racial and social matrix, the increasing
dependence on a matriarchy for several generations of child care
and child rearing, and the death of Mary. Without climax or resolution, the text suspends itself in the exchange of gazes: the
reader-spectator's of Sister Mary; Mary's of the camera and the
out-of-focus beyond. In the exchange, death as the primary
transformation is also momentarily suspended. Sweet Flypaper,
thus, may be read not only as a narrative of process, a chronicle
of change, but also as a production occurring between the moment of the announcement of change and the moment of recognition of subject named in the actualization of change. It unites
the familiarities of voice and image, self-representation and communal representation, in a final moment before fictional vision
confronts the unknown and the unthinkable thereafter.

WORKS CITED

Bradley, David. Introduction to *Twelve Million Black Voices*. New York: Thunder's Mouth Press, 1988.

Hughes, Langston, and Roy DeCarava. *The Sweet Flypaper of Life*. 1955. Rpt. New York: Hill & Wang, 1967.

Miller, R. Baxter. *The Art and Imagination of Langston Hughes.* Lexington: University Press of Kentucky, 1989.

Rampersad, Arnold. *The Life of Langston Hughes; Volume II: 1941–1967: I Dream A World*, 2 vols. New York: Oxford University Press, 1988.

Wright, Richard. *Twelve Million Black Voices.* Photo direction by Edwin Rosskam. 1941. Rpt. New York: Thunder's Mouth Press, 1988.

The Man and His Continuing Influence

Hughes's Personal Library and Exhibits (*Special Collections, Langston Hughes Memorial Library, Lincoln University*)

Sophy H. Cornwell
Lincoln University

On the first page of his autobiography, *The Big Sea*, Langston Hughes wrote: "Melodramatic, maybe, it seems to me now. But then it was like throwing a million bricks out of my heart when I threw the books into the water. I leaned over the rail . . . and threw the books I had had at Columbia and those books I had lately bought to read."

It is difficult to believe that Langston Hughes ever threw *anything* out, as I'm certain Dr. Rampersad discovered in researching his biography of Hughes. Lincoln University is only one of the many institutions that benefitted from Hughes's generosity. In his will he stated, "I give and bequeath to Lincoln University my entire library of books in the English language, including those which I have authored and all magazines, phamphlets (sic), booklets, paperback books and newspapers of research value."

As the several dozen boxes arrived at Lincoln in 1968, we found that the bequest consisted of more than 3300 items. Of the books, not all are in the English language (note the copy of *Not Without Laughter* in Chinese in the display of *Langston Hughes Fiction*), some are in French, Spanish, etc. Many of the books are annotated by Hughes; some are presentation copies from other authors. A reading of the inscriptions shows that Hughes's literary friends and acquaintances were many and varied. His assistance to and inspiration of other writers are evident in their tributes to him. A few of the autographed presentation copies are on display in the section devoted to Hughes's personal library. Also in that section is a copy of the book *Poems* by Frances E.W. Harper that belonged to Langston's father.

In addition to the types of materials mentioned in his will, Lincoln University was fortunate to receive an extensive collection of memorabilia. As mentioned before, Hughes must not have thrown anything away—there are airline schedules, postcards (enough to fill numerous pages in an album that was purchased to preserve them), travel folders, programs from his many appearances throughout the United States, and a souvenir stamp album from the First World Festival of Negro Arts held in Dakar in April 1966, mentioned by Dr. Rampersad in his speech this morning.

Hughes's interest in Africa and the Caribbean, themes he often used in his writings, is also represented in his library. Books, small volumes of poetry (many autographed) written by authors from Nigeria, Jamaica, Trinidad, Cuba, by both obscure and well-known authors such as Chinua Achebe, Wole Soyinka, and V.S. Naipaul, are among those in the collection.

One of the most touching foreign publications is *Lament for Dark Peoples,* which is a collection of Hughes's poetry published in Holland under the German occupation during World War II. In a letter to Hughes dated February 17, 1946, which accompanied a copy of the book (which is on display), the publisher apologizes for having published the collection of poems without Hughes's permission. He said, "I did something I ought not to have done. . . . But I thought it more important to publish poetry from a Negro poet in English in full wartime being under German occupation, than to bother about if the author would approve or not." He also mentions that the profit from the sale of the book (by necessity a limited edition) was only about $100 and that he was told that "you do not care very much about money . . . although . . . you are not a rich man." An offer of $50 was made to Hughes as a share of the profit.

A survey of the contents of Langston Hughes's personal library stored in the cases in this area and in the three file cabinets also in this room is a constant delightful surprise. To be expected are the books by his contemporaries of the Harlem Renaissance and after—Arna Bontemps, Zora Neale Hurston, Countee Cullen, and others. Interspersed with these authors can be found titles from *Winnie the Pooh* to the *Autobiography of Malcolm X*, a book on card tricks, more than one copy of the Bible, *Poems for What Ails You*. Something for everyone, and it seems Hughes was interested in everything.

Of Langston Hughes and Lincoln: Although he had already published *The Weary Blues* by the time he enrolled in Lincoln in 1927, there is not a great deal to document his stay. Except for the few items that are on exhibit in one of the cases in the lobby, the sociology paper he wrote with two of his classmates, "Three Students Look at Lincoln" (on display)—incidentally, he saved all the questionnaires and research done for the project, 129 items—and some poems that appeared in the campus newspaper, few records of his presence survive in the University Archives or his collections other than his chapters about his Lincoln days in *The Big Sea*. Dr. Rampersad's extensive chapter, "A Lion at Lincoln" and the following chapter in his biography of Hughes supply a number of new insights into what life was like for Hughes at Lincoln from 1927 to 1929.

Hughes did publish his second volume of poems while at Lincoln, *Fine Clothes to the Jew*, and in the summer after both his junior and senior years he worked on and completed *Not Without Laughter*. That Lincoln held a special place in Hughes's affections throughout his life is attested to by his many visits to the campus, his part in the compilation of the *Lincoln University Centennial Anthology* (1954), for which he wrote a special poem, and his presence as the featured speaker at the Omega Psi Phi Golden Anniversary Celebration in 1964. The most important evidence of his devotion to Lincoln is the gift of his personal library as a lasting memorial.

And for Langston Hughes there is a special place in the hearts and minds of Lincoln men and women, both alumni and those of us who have spent a part of our lives here, for through his life and his writing he has helped us to

> . . . dream a world where man no other man will scorn,
> Where love will bless the earth

And peace its path adorn.
A world I dream where black and white,
Whatever race you be,
Will *share* the bounties of the earth
And every man is free.
Of such I dream—
Our world!

Hughes as Dramatist

Ella Forbes
Temple University

The performance we have just witnessed—seven excerpts of Hughes's twelve plays—and enjoyed is a wonderful, rousing and fitting finale to this conference organized to celebrate Langston Hughes, the man and the writer. The excerpts illustrate the most compelling attribute of the man and the writer: his accessibility. Not only did he write in easy to understand language, but as a man, he was, from all reports a person easy to approach. This was, of course, because he loved his people with a love evident in his work.

Langston wrote in a manner designed to speak to, for, and from African Americans, and we recognize ourselves, our triumphs, and our failures in his work. In other words, he gives voice to our concerns. He wrote in a manner, as the performance's introductory piece says, designed to portray what it means to be an African American in this nation by placing us historically. And because he places us historically, his work is clearly art for propaganda's sake. He has a political message. His art, then, serves as an indictment against the America that never was.

One of the central themes of Hughes's work is African American resistance to oppressive situations. Most of the pieces we saw tonight are examples of African American resistance. And because Hughes is an accessible writer, he often uses humor and easily identifiable cultural motifs to depict this resistance.

167

Simply Heavenly uses comedy and a mother wit very famil-iar to African Americans in order to expose illogical and inexpli-cable white racism. Hughes, through Simple, is speaking directly to the fact that the armed forces had recently been supposedly integrated and to the incongruity inherent in requiring military service from men who did not enjoy full citizenship. The folk so-cial commentator, Simple, says, "You are me and I am you and we are one. And now that our fighting is done, let's be Ameri-cans for once."

Jericho-Jim Crow celebrates African American resistance more directly by listing important participants in the Civil Rights Movement. Because he only gives us abbreviated names, Hughes makes it clear that we should know and celebrate our heroes. We, of course, know of Dr. Martin Luther King Jr. and Rev. Ralph Abernathy, but do we remember and acknowledge the contributions of Daisy Bates, who led the integration of Central High in Little Rock, Arkansas, and Charlayne Hunter-Gault, who integrated the University of Georgia?

We are also familiar with Robert in *Mulatto*. To us, Robert is a symbol of the "dual consciousness" which so often afflicts African Americans. He represents the dichotomy intrinsic in a nation which espouses democratic ideals while oppressing a portion of its citizenry. Robert's resistance to his situation leads him to a self-destructive, but ultimately liberating end. However, as a panelist said today, we must question Robert's assumption that it is his white blood, rather than his humanity, which should guarantee his rights. Unfortunately, the excerpt is too short to cover the ending, but because Langston Hughes is an accessible writer, the ending is what one would expect. From the opening scene, it is apparent that Robert and Willie will be destroyed by racism. The play instantly reminds us of two of Hughes's poems, "Mulatto" and "Cross," which deal with the same issue as does the short story, "Father and Son."

The resistance to oppression is very obvious in *Don't You Want to Be Free?* The speech the young man gives at the end of the piece states this explicitly. "Some of us always carried on our fight and kept alive the seeds of revolt." Again, we are asked to celebrate African American heroes when Hughes names them: Nat Turner, Denmark Vesey, Harriet Tubman, and Sojourner

Truth. This piece also establishes historical African American resistance which occurred with the first imposition of the condition of enslavement.

The humorous, but sorrowful, *Soul Gone Home,* which was shown in its entirety, is the story of the effects of overwhelming poverty. The ability to truly love has been crushed out of the mother. She simply acts or mimes feelings and life. That the poverty has some racial implications is evident in the mother's concern that white men will see her dead child act up.

The gospel play, *Prodigal Son,* is an obvious biblical allegory set in Harlem. And the other gospel play, *Tambourines to Glory,* represents some unsavory aspects of the African American religious experience—the proliferation of storefront churches and the damage that the abuse of religious principles can cause. Because Hughes is an accessible and honest writer, he does not avoid the unpleasant issue in this play. The gender issue is another theme of *Tambourines to Glory* and is reminiscent of many of his "Lament over Love" poems.

All of the excerpts show Langston Hughes's versatility as a writer, his concern with racial and social issues, and his understanding of historical reality. In his well-known and often quoted essay, "The Negro and the Racial Mountain," Langston Hughes explains his commitment to an African American aesthetic: "The road for the serious black artist who would produce a racial art is most certainly rocky and the mountain is high." He goes on to say: "Without going outside his race and even among the better classes with their "white" culture and conscious American manners, but still Negro enough to be different, there is sufficient matter to furnish a black artist with a lifetime of creative work." Langston Hughes, the man and the writer, certainly scaled the mountain, built his temple for tomorrow, and lived up to his ideal.

Index